The Stewardship Call

Waldo J. Werning

The Stewardship Call

An approach to personal and group stewardship based on the concept of Christian vocation

Concordia Publishing House
Saint Louis

Acknowledgments

The author and publisher acknowledge that the following have granted permission to reprint the following copyrighted material.

From *Your Money and Your Church*, copyright 1959 by Richard Byfield and James P. Shaw. Reprinted by permission of Doubleday & Company Incorporated.

From *Servants and Stewards* by Arthur McKay, page 25, copyright 1963, W. L. Jenkins. The Geneva Press. Used by permission.

From *The Institutional Nature of Adult Christian Education* by Bruce Reinhart, pp. 16 and 23, copyright 1962, W. L. Jenkins. The Westminster Press. Used by permission.

Preface

Short-range stewardship efforts seem to have created a false confidence and have led some congregations to believe that their stewardship problems are being solved. Outward successes tend to conceal the weaknesses of the basic stewardship structure so that sufficient efforts are not undertaken for the long-range tasks which are inherent in Christian stewardship. Stewardship should be "God's show," so to speak, and we will do well to recognize how it can deteriorate into a "sideshow" put on by man.

This book presents a theological foundation for stewardship and shows the relation of this theology to stewardship messages and methods. The varied possibilities of stewardship interpretation and action will be investigated according to the nature of the church's basic mission. Then ways will be sought by which the fulness of each believer's ministry can be embodied in stewardship efforts.

We propose a new foundation as the basis of stewardship. The concept of the Christian vocation is explored in its many facets. This study is not a negative critique of the stewardship movement; it even goes beyond a positive and constructive critique, for it offers a working theology of stewardship with all its implications for the church of our day. We attempt to define afresh the theological concepts of stewardship, and then we consider the tensions and traditions of the church as we apply Biblical stewardship principles to the life and practice of the church.

We are not concerned with stewardship practices of the church at large but specifically with the local parish scene and with individuals. Written for leaders of congregations, the focus is not limited to one denomination but includes Protestantism in general.

Many pastors and laymen in varying degrees already hold to both the theology and the practice which this book embraces and discusses. Some of these men have been generous assistants and kind friends in helping the author in his personal growth in stewardship understanding in the past 15 years. Some have had a strategic part in the interplay that goes on between workers engaged in the tasks of the kingdom and active in producing a book of this nature. The author's tender years of faltering steps in stewardship efforts were made easy through the kind assistance and guidance of Dr. John E. Herrmann as an associate for 4½ years and as a co-worker for 14 years — a distinct advantage that few people may experience. This book carries the theme of grace that he has taught so well.

Some men gave special encouragement toward growth and craftsmanship needed in a discipline as strategic as stewardship. The Rev. Ellis Nieting has been a faithful personal counselor toward understanding the magnitude of the theological considerations in stewardship. Biblical perspective was provided generously by the Rev. Alvin Hornbostel. There has been the regular tossing of the ball back and forth in an exchange of ideas, especially with the Rev. Reuben Schmidt and the Rev. Carl Hiller. Men who have graciously spent many hours providing enrichment with their thoughts and experiences include Leslie Allenstein, the Rev. Alfred Ernst, the Rev. Cal Fiege, and many others. The contribution by Dr. T. K. Thompson, Executive Director of the Department of Stewardship and Benevolences of the National Council of Churches of Christ in the U.S.A., has been substantial through personal contacts and correspondence over the years.

Biblical quotations are from the King James and Revised Standard Versions except where a different translation is indicated.

For the Gospel's sake we trust that this exercise of our stewardship will stimulate the stewardship of our readers.

Waldo J. Werning

Table of Contents

The Stewardship Call

Chapter 1

The Stewardship Question

The seeming ineffectiveness of getting at *primary* steward-ship problems indicates that something basic is missing. Many pastors and leaders desire to take the step that would get them out of the "stewardship forest," but they are not quite certain what that step is. There is no magic way out, but there are numerous steps of study and review that will lead to better stewardship paths.

The theory of stewardship has been in evidence in many ways, but it appears that there is a lack of prudent applica-tion of the theology of stewardship to actual practice on the parish level. Stewardship seems to be regarded too much as a project or program to be promoted periodically. It finds many churchmen improvising solutions to problems which are not the real problems at all.

There is no question about the progress many congrega-tions have made in their stewardship and giving efforts. Many of the progressive steps were taken with concern for proper spiritual growth. Denominational headquarters have provided some excellent aids which have been instrumental in such growth. Yet crucial issues are still evident everywhere. Many questions call for more permanent answers.

Some past patterns of message and method have evolved from one step of popularity to another, regardless of their merit or nature. It is particularly disturbing when a new pastor completely reverses the stewardship message and prac-tice of his predecessor — to the confusion and bewilderment of the membership. In varying degrees congregations have experienced a change in stewardship practices simply be-cause of a change of pastors. This has been particularly true of Christian giving.

Looking Back at Stewardship Patterns in Giving

The European background had its effect on American giving habits for many years. Many Protestants, especially Lutherans, came from tax-supported state churches where there were no regular offerings. With that background, churches in America for many years did not concern themselves with a Biblical study of Christian giving. Neither European nor American theologians addressed themselves to the study of Christian giving and its Biblical theology. Consequently pastors and leaders of congregations adopted the best methods of giving they knew; accepted practices which seemed best for them as the need arose. The apparent need for giving was underscored by salaries that had to be paid, churches that were to be built, bills for heat, repairs, Communion supplies, and other needs. Appeals were made to all members to do their share meeting expenses. Prior to adopting regular budgets, in some church bodies members contributed to various funds of the denomination (general administration, India or China, church college, etc.). As needs arose, they were put before the people. Individuals then gave or pledged a certain amount to help cover the needs. And there were the ever-present "benefits," sales, and bazaars to help finance the church.

In many areas churches employed forms of taxation for raising funds. There were various methods; some were outright, while others were quite subtle. Sometimes families were assigned arbitrary quotas according to their holdings, or they were asked to raise a certain amount per family, disregarding variations in their incomes. Even in recent years such forms of taxation have been practiced in some congregations.

The church then shifted from forms of taxation to needs, which still was only a short way from taxation, but it represented an attempt to be fair. The needs were covered by pledges and payments of "dues." Everyone was to do his "share." Much of this was arbitrary. "Do we give another $10 when the pledges do not underwrite the local budget and all are asked to raise their pledge a little?" Averages and fair shares were stressed. At times there were emotional appeals to bring out an additional dollar for reaching another poor heathen. "The Lord hath need" was the favorite chorus to get just a little more money.

While there has been a shift to weekly offerings and envelopes, the need and the budget are still prime considerations. It has not been seriously considered that even in "emergency giving," as in the case of the charitable effort of the Jerusalem Christians, the need is cited as an incidental factor to the great underlying principle of motivation ("Ye know the grace of our Lord Jesus Christ, etc."). We are all still plagued with money-raising schemes and numerous special drives.

Usually, financial policies with their history of ineffective support have been geared to what we term a *"starvation" policy:* there are so many dollars people will give, and each interest group must inspire members for its own cause or the money will not be given. Those who send out the best leaders and use the best materials have been getting the most dollars; actually, each cause has had to vie with others — missions against home, home against charities, church charities against public charities, building funds against missions — one against the other. Competition for the church member's dollar among churches, religious organizations, and other charitable groups has often been conducted on a level that removes giving from the area of a spiritual grace. Such collections usually are not conducted in a way that a person can have adequate knowledge as to how to divide his offerings, and the competitive programs have evidenced much substandard motivation and have often been on the level of humanistic promotion.

The day of the starvation procedure finds the church suffering from financial shortages at a time when income, spending, and savings are higher than ever before. Churches have been in the financial straitjacket of the starvation "squeeze" for years, and in many places this plight is getting worse in a time of plenty and when church fund raising has been elevated to something of a science. In the midst of it all many churches do not seem to be able to get the real message across to God's people — many of them are not getting the point.

The techniques under the so-called starvation policy indicate that fund raising has become a set procedure with "proven" results. Many parish leaders deny it but still abide by this policy: even under the unified plan they stuff as many envelopes into the box as will fit; for Easter they provide the regular Sunday envelope plus the colorful Easter envelope, both going to the unified budget! (While community leaders must plead needs, they are to be commended for organizing the United Fund, and careful planning is required of all groups so that people do not face endless appeals to give to all types of individual causes.)

Idolizing Traditional Patterns

The church is being crowded into a corner at a time when it faces unending needs in the world. Not all stewardship problems can be excused by blaming materialism and secularism. As the church's demands mount, we ask: "What type of claim does the institution or congregation have on the individual member?" We are not concerned with the negative criticism leveled against the institution, for the criticism may be only a smokescreen for evading responsible participation in the tasks of the Kingdom. We are concerned with helping those who seek to define their problems and who search for positive solutions.

Stewardship leaders will want to assure themselves that they are not dealing only with the "plugging of holes" or "fixing worn-out fences" instead of constructing a permanent educational approach. Some efforts may gain temporary results but leave the church weaker in the end.

As Luther's Reformation activities had the vital interest of

14

setting the religion of God over against the religion of men, so our searching must set the ways of God over against the ways of men in stewardship. This vital task of the continuing Reformation is not destructive but constructive. It seeks not to tear down but to build up.

Questions of Stewardship Lights and Shadows

Some stewardship practices bring spiritual vigor to parish life while others prevent or discourage healthy growth in sanctification and the expression of faith. There are lights and shadows in this matter. The lights of stewardship knowledge and resultant activity are gained from God's Word. Shadows are cast on Scriptural stewardship precepts by blindly following traditional patterns without reference to their merit or validity. The church member may by faithful stewardship serve God, or he may by haphazard giving and a self-willed life cast shadows on the stewardship life.

Questions ought to be asked about the lights and shadows of *motivation*. What appeals are to be used to inspire people to an active Christian life? Certain motives may be suggested that may help to get immediate results but which may do much harm in the long pull of church work. Can there be proper appeals to loyalty and pride? Is the payment of church bills a good motivation? Does prosperity ever create a greater sense of stewardship? What is the nature and use of the Law and the Gospel in urging the dedicated life?

What are the lights and shadows in *objectives and goals?* The plans of the institution are to be used properly. Are institutional goals primary or subordinate means? Does leadership have a responsibility beyond the enlistment of talents for church offices and positions? What is the church's task — to raise money or men or both? Are prebudget educational programs the proper approach or is the budget to be projected so that people might know what is needed? Has success been achieved when budgets have been increased and exceeded? Is the only concern one of seeing a change in giving habits? Is there a place for fair shares and apportionments? What stress should be placed upon firstfruits, giving in worship, and proportionate giving? Is the Every Member Stewardship Visit (EMSV) successful because pledges meet projected needs? Can it be said that a congregation ever goes "over the top" in its financial efforts?

Concerning *methods*, a balanced stress should be put upon organization and procedure. The content of the stewardship message must be evaluated. Is it necessary for everyone to participate in the work of the church and to pledge? In what ways can leaders impose their will upon others and manipulate people in ways that do more harm than good? Is it necessary to take the message into the home or can it be done at group meetings in the church? Can the educational program be left to the pastor in the pulpit? What are the alternatives to sporadic, short-run programs? How basic is a good cultivation program for Christian growth? Should Christians pledge a percentage or a certain amount of their income?

Theology Must Set the Stewardship Base and the Structure

What are the facts, factors, and forces which will help overcome problems and weaknesses in the stewardship movement? Knowing these will help us avoid programing solely to overcome symptoms — a waste of time and energy. Many ventures allow a choice of starting places and routes to travel. In stewardship there is only *one* starting place: Biblical theology. It is the task of theology to interpret the essential nature, meaning, and purpose of the Gospel for the life of the church: its function is also to judge what is wrong or missing.

The theology of stewardship is the discipline which seeks to relate the Gospel in the depth and fulness of its meaning to stewardship. It is the means by which the church is able to learn something about its dilemma between the doctrine of the priesthood of all believers and its programs, between a theology of grace and organizational demands for production. Being human and in a sinful world, God's workers are beset by temptations to dilute the Gospel with human inventions.

Since many congregations appear to have a stewardship program without a clear theological base, leaders should ask these searching questions: Where are we now? How did we get here? Where do we hope to go? What shall we do to get there? What can we learn from the Word of God and history? Are we ready to apply crucial tests so that we might determine the relevance and usefulness of all our efforts? Are we willing to cut and prune without respect to personalities? Are we prepared to step out boldly into new stewardship ventures according to the dictates of our theology? How can a well-defined theology of stewardship contribute to a more meaningful church life?

These chapters will attempt to indicate the unity which should be found in the theology, messages, and methods of stewardship emphases. The present scene often finds them in competition or forced together into a contrived situation. Theology should speak to all situations in order to clear away some of the debris of the activistic storms which have surrounded some of our church life. The concept and practice of stewardship is to grow out of the nature of Christianity (God's relation to man) and of the purpose and mission of the Christian church.

Some people believe that they have an effective and spiritual program with a good theological base when they have done little more than to take questionable, traditional methods and justify them with a few Bible verses. Some assertions about Bible-based and Christ-centered programs reveal a topical use of the Bible without evidence of true Biblical orientation.

Stewardship activities, like all practices, are derived. It is a question of what they are derived from. How do we hope to arrive at our ultimate stewardship concept and approach? Theology provides the criteria for such judgment and observation. Theology provides the base and direction, and it allows for the spelling out of basic principles.

Various crises have pushed many a congregation to feverish stewardship activity from time to time. Significantly, both the "need" had existed and the commission of Christ had been known before the crisis arose, but no action was taken. Why should it take a financial crisis to bring into action a concerted effort to do what the church should have been doing all along? The study of the theology of stewardship will discourage groups from hopping from one crisis to another, and it will assist in the formation of a program that emerges from the Biblical base.

A Definition

Christian stewardship is the believer's response to God's love in creating, preserving, redeeming, and sanctifying him. It can be called the Christian's management of his redeemed life and possessions, by the Spirit's power and direction through the Word — to God's glory and for man's benefit. Christian stewardship is the fruit of saving faith. It is faith in action, the expression of the Christian faith, the evidence of how sincerely the child of God believes the truths he embraces. A Christian steward is a person who is entrusted with a life redeemed by Christ. To be a steward is to follow where God leads by the abilities and the strength He gives.

Stewardship theology provides all the underlying principles for the believers' management of their lives. The succeeding chapters speak to this issue. It is a fascinating story which starts with God's relation to man, but also looks at man's nature and his motivations.

Chapter 2

The Stewardship Struggle

Life parades many good and exciting things before our view. Their acquisition, however, provides only fleeting days of joy. Those who stake everything on material possessions in due time discover to their dismay that their possessions are like vapor in the wind. The struggle of life is weakly discerned and understood by human eyes and minds.

Charles Malik, eminent Christian statesman and teacher, describes the struggle that goes on within us. He writes: "We struggle on at least six fronts. We struggle, first, on the front of the world and its temptations, this world which is so exciting, so colorful, so seductive, so sweet, that we are always in danger of losing ourselves in it and forgetting about Jesus Christ. We struggle, second, against our own memories, those strange whisperings in the dark which ever want to keep us captive to themselves. We struggle, third, against our sweet, natural tendency to be lazy and slothful, to covet more than we need, to expect from life more than we give it. We struggle, fourth, against our inveterate pride, that creaturely raising of ourselves above ourselves, that blasphemous pitting of ourselves against God, that pitiful refusal to let go — in humor, in brokenness, and in tears. We struggle, fifth, against our daily fall in the worship of things and objects — the worship of ourselves, our possessions, our country, our culture; in short, against the worship of perishing and corrupt creatures, whose meaning can never be understood apart from the living God who created them. Finally, we struggle daily against the devil himself; the devil who always lures us by the three temptations of security, magic, and power; the devil who almost succeeds — in fact, apart from the repeated interventions of Christ, he always does succeed — in *proving* to us that there is no God, no Christ, and no Holy Spirit." [1]

Unless we as stewards understand our dual natures, how the old nature and the new nature in Christ struggle against each other, we will be unduly confused.

Before the Struggle

Before Christ renewed us, we were slaves to sin. The old Adam, our inborn corruption, is one of the consequences of sin. In Romans, chapters 5 to 8, and in Galatians, chapter 5, we learn about the persistence of the old nature but also about the believer's victory through the power of the Gospel. The old nature remains in us as a legacy of sin.

The devil encourages our old Adam to assert himself. Even under our most favorable conditions Satan is powerful and active. We are fit subjects for him in our inherent nature: depraved, selfish, intellectually lazy, intoxicated with entertainment, and limited in spiritual outlook. Luther put it this way: "spiritually blind, dead, and an enemy of God."

We like to point to the enemy outside as the reason for our failures. Our old Adam is so dull and spiritually blind that he cannot see his inconsistencies. The "Pharisee" within us points in many directions but never inside. He maintains a form of godliness which cloaks him with respectability so that he can accuse everyone of being out of step except himself.

Foolish sentiments, natural affections, wild fancies, and pet notions are poisonous. As natural man is allowed to go uncontrolled and undisciplined in his self-seeking piety, the Christian life suffers. The old Adam sees, seeks, and thinks about himself in all things. He causes us to seek ways by which we may bypass grace and walk on our own. The old man rejects the forgiving Word as the only effective remedy for our problems.

Christians who do not clearly perceive their sinful nature will have difficulty in understanding the Christian life and stewardship in its true light. Sinful man likes to pamper himself, and so he dilutes the Gospel in its relation to his own needs. To the extent that we pamper ourselves, seek prominence, resent others, love praise, resist correction, and put on a mask of piety, to that extent we hinder and short-circuit the power of the living Christ.

Birth of the Struggle

God took drastic steps to change the course of our lives. He imparted to us His own goodness and prepared salvation through Jesus Christ for all men. By His incarnation, death, and resurrection Christ is the source and goal of the new life for all who trust in Him.

Our union with Christ and our life of discipleship is the consequence of our Baptism in Christ. Baptism makes us a part of His body, His church, in which each of us stands in vital relationship to the Lord and to each other. The daily reminder of the baptismal covenant of grace is necessary for an active Christian life. St. Paul says, "that like as Christ was raised up from the dead by the glory of the Father, even so we also should walk in newness of life." (Rom. 6:4)

We should see our entire life in the perspective of our Baptism. That which you and I received through Baptism and the Spirit is not just another gift of life — it is Life, it is Christ, it is His Lordship. By the power of Baptism we are renewed and consecrated for the service of God.

We contribute as little to our spiritual birth as we do to our physical. As a carpenter cannot make a tree, so we cannot produce the rebirth. God causes the Word, the Gospel, as a seed to be planted and to grow in our hearts. When this seed finds root in our hearts, the Holy Spirit makes a new man.

We have no true moral power on which we may depend unless we are re-created and renewed within through the Spirit of Christ. In this act God neither forces nor sets aside our will but, after regeneration, enables and guides us in making right choices. Apart from the love of God in Christ Jesus, we choose to keep God out of our life by arranging and handling things our own way. Through Baptism and the

Gospel our life is one of assured forgiveness of sins and renewal; by the removal of the guilt of sin we are taken into fellowship with Christ.

When God speaks forgiveness through His Word, an exchange of rulers takes place in our life. The old "I" no longer reigns, but Christ. "For as by one man's disobedience many were made sinners, so by the obedience of one shall many be made righteous. . . . That as sin hath reigned unto death, even so might grace reign through righteousness unto eternal life by Jesus Christ, our Lord" (Rom. 5:19,21). In that fact lies the secret of our strength and direction as stewards.

Baptism assures us forgiveness so we can break through our barriers and love as God has loved us. Karl Barth says: "We live by forgiveness." Because we exist by the assurance of God's grace, "we no longer have to pretend a holiness we do not have. We can acknowledge our subtle arrogance, our little deceits, our eagerness to escape responsibility, and all the rest of our sins." [2] Growing piety comes from the forgiveness experienced through union with Christ.

No personal relationship of real value is possible except it exists by forgiveness, for the nature of sin is so horrible that it blinds people to God's activity of love to them and to others. A right understanding of forgiveness, offered by God to people and between people, is essential to the management or stewardship of our life. A wrong understanding of this life of forgiveness leads us into an arid desert of pharisaic deeds and an outward form of religion. The facts of God's dealings with sin, justifying us by faith through Christ, cannot be ignored in the formulation of a concept and message of Christian stewardship. Without a focus on forgiveness from God and between men, we will have stewardship messages and programs which are divorced from the realities of the Gospel and of the power of Baptism. The daily life of forgiveness will keep the steward from regarding himself as right with God just because he thinks he has fulfilled God's will by his stewardship acts. God's acts of forgiveness and renewal in

Christ are the heart of the Gospel, and the Gospel is at the heart of stewardship.

Christ shapes the motives and conduct of all who are united with Him. This is known from John 15:5: "I am the Vine, ye are the branches; he that abideth in Me, and I in him, the same bringeth forth much fruit." Believers are branches that have been grafted into Christ, and from Him they receive their new life. From Him who produces life and fruit we draw our ability to bear fruit. What sustains and directs this union is illustrated by the life of the Vine. Christ's life-giving energy surges through all the branches to give them His vitality and purposefulness.

Paul brings into clear focus the renewal, design, and power for our lives when he tells of "spiritual corpses" becoming truly alive to the purposes of God (Eph. 2). Man is not saved by the fruits of his life or by his good works: "For by grace are ye saved through faith; and that not of yourselves, it is the gift of God; not of works, lest any man should boast" (vv. 8,9). Then why do good works? Not in order to become alive or to be saved, but simply because we are alive in Christ! Eph. 2:10 shows that we are God's handiwork fashioned for production — made to serve and glorify Him. To expect fruit and stewardship acts from an individual who is not attached to Christ's life in faith is to expect something impossible and unreasonable.

Theodore Heimarck explains what happens through Christ's indwelling. He says: "What is really offered is not only something done *for* us but *in* us. The cross is a way of life that allows the Saviorhood of Christ to result in citizenship in the Kingdom over which He reigns. It is, as Scripture says, a death to self, so that it can be said that 'It is no longer I who live, but Christ who lives in me.' This, good friends, is a terrifying thought. I know I keep twisting and squirming away from a personal Golgotha that means death to *my* choices, *my* decisions, *my* protective and indulgent care of self. . . . It is the death of the 'I' and 'my' that Jesus demands, and

23

there can be no newness of life until human bodies become the temples of his Spirit." [3]

The Reality of the Struggle

The old nature remains old to the very end. The new nature is not a change, reformation, or stimulation of the old nature, but an impartation of a new nature which in God is created in righteousness and holiness. The new man arises as the old man is daily put to death.

St. Paul in 1 Cor. 12 and Eph. 4 portrays what happens when by faith men become members of the body of Christ and He becomes their Head. The Head transmits its impulses, love, and will to the members of the body. Christian response is not something artificial, something forced by mechanical means, but the natural, spontaneous function of the members of the body. The will, once self-centered and fixed on earthly things only, grows more and more close to the will of Christ until finally in heaven it will be completely and permanently identified with it. The newness expresses itself in tender sensitivity, highly tempered flexibility, simple directness, infinite patience, compassionate love, deep humility, and complete dependence upon the God of promise.

In receiving us into grace God delivers us from egocentricity, but the inner war wages on. The flesh (self-rule) struggles constantly against the new nature (God-rule), a tension which exists as long as we live. Even though forgiven, we live out our service to God and neighbor with a double identity in the tension of the old nature against the new. Even though the old nature is continually mortified, it is never completely eradicated.

Two inner drives strive for mastery over us. The old man is subject to deceit in contrast to the new man who is in truth. It is characteristic of the old man to desire things wrongly for himself while the new man looks with concern on the affairs of others. The old man is in accord with the nature of

24

the sinful world in contrast to the new man who is in accord with God.

The old and the new coexist; one is progressively being overwhelmed and conquered by Christ while the other is constantly growing and developing into maturity in Christ. The old must daily be put down with the Law. The believer, in whom the new man reigns, is empowered by the Gospel to be a functioning member of the body of Christ. Therefore, St. Paul speaks of "putting off" the old and "putting on" the new man: *"Put off* your old nature which belongs to your former manner of life and is corrupt through deceitful lusts, and be renewed in the spirit of your minds, and *put on* the new nature, created after the likeness of God in true righteousness and holiness"* (Eph. 4:22-24 RSV). *"Put on* the new man, which is renewed in knowledge after the image of Him that created him." (Col. 3:10)

Luther says: "To be both old man and new means to be one who is sick, in whom illness and health contend. One cannot mechanically identify which is which in the actions of a convalescent." [4]

The conflict between the old and new life makes each of us a "sinner-saint." Luther uses the phrase "righteous and sinful at the same time." Kantonen writes: "To say that a justified believer is both a sinner and a saint does not mean that he is partly a sinner, partly a saint. In himself he is altogether a sinner, in Christ he is altogether a saint. Justification stresses the former aspect, sanctification the latter. Justification stands for the truth that without the grace of forgiveness man is nothing but a sinner, sanctification for the truth that 'where there is forgiveness of sins, there is life.'" [5] The Christian should learn to know when the "natural man" is pushing and when the "Christ-in-him" is leading.

There is a distortion of the CHRIST-ian faith if it is treated from the saint's side alone or as if it were concerned only with spiritual things. Physical factors and material blessings should not be minimized, for they come from God. They

25

are not to be divorced from the spiritual life; in fact they cannot be separated. The spiritual aspects of life affect the material. God Himself has joined the two together and resolved the tension between them in the person of His Son, Jesus. Through Christ we are enabled to live in the Spirit and thus control material things for the good of man and the glory of God. Material things in themselves should not be denounced nor made to seem wicked and perverse, for through Christ they can in a sense be "redeemed" for Him. The entire world, including the material, has been created by God, and hence there can be no sharp distinction for Christians between the spiritual and the material. It is the way we use things that causes trouble.

The CHRIST-ian has been assured of victory in the struggles of his dual nature. While in a sense it is true that we Christians seek victory, the fact remains that we live and work *from* victory — from the victory which is ours by virtue of Christ's victory announced in the Gospel. In the resurrection of Christ all powers and dominions which held us captive have been overpowered and their authority taken away. When we are "in Christ," we are free from sin's tyranny, for we belong to another Master. We are partakers of Christ's triumph. Satan is a defeated foe. In confidence we affirm what God has already affirmed: "We are more than conquerors through Him that loved us." (Rom. 8:37)

We live on resurrection ground. On that ground we can face any temptation; we can patiently bear any privation; we can cope with any task or difficulty. The "Civil War" is won! To be sure, grave battles are to be faced in our struggles, but the persistent old man has already been defeated. We are working *from* victory, not *for* victory. In reality we work *from* victory *to* victory, working only to claim and proclaim the victory.

God's design for the new life is also the blueprint for Christian stewardship. The new man's triumph and power over the old man is the gateway to a mountain-removing, world-conquering faith that is more than a future hope. This stewardship concept will lead to a recognition of the potentialities of the Christian life and of the church.

Strength for the Struggle

Many modern institutions teach us how to make a living. The Word gives life and teaches us how to live. Man's philosophies and beliefs offer an assortment of tranquilizers for people filled with fear. We are so easily monopolized by the physical side of life and distracted from the spiritual. In the means of grace God offers the only stabilizer to strengthen feeble knees and provide a sure foundation on which to build one's destiny.

Worship, preaching, Bible study and devotions, Baptism and Holy Communion — through all these means God is calling man to Himself and is keeping him true to his calling. Faith that is fed by the food God offers will prove its vitality and constancy in growth or sanctification.

The stewardship task is to get people to see the real problem of their existence, which is hidden behind a complex of difficulties, both personal and congregational. The message should raise questions, present illustrations, and bring warnings and admonitions from the Bible which are calculated to point out the areas that people need to know in order to fulfill their ministry of service and giving. Because stewardship is so full of slogans and catchwords, it needs nothing as much as to hear the voice of God from His stewardship spokesmen.

The Christian's moral power and spiritual vitality come from the life-creating Spirit through the Word. This work in the believer's life enlightens the understanding and puts things into their proper relation. The Holy Spirit is the Power who enters human life by faith and delivers man from enslavement to Satan, sin, and death. What the Holy Spirit *begins* dramatically in man, He also *continues*. The Christian life and stewardship is made possible in a man born of the

27

Spirit, walking in the Spirit, led by the Spirit, and filled with the Spirit. The Holy Spirit not only makes the Christian a conqueror of natural weaknesses but also gives him willingness and direction to follow God's call. The quickening Spirit gives the impulse and the ability for fruitful living.

A person may know the words and doctrines of the Bible, but unless he is filled with the Spirit he will find his life filled with conflict and defeat, spiritual infancy, and fruitlessness. Few things are more pathetic than a church member trying to "turn on the heat" to build up his enthusiasm by his own intelligence and strength without laying hold of the power of the Spirit.

The Holy Spirit is the Great Transformer. He changes weakness to power, bad dispositions to pleasant attitudes, self-centeredness to Christ-likeness, self-reasoning to Christ-mindedness. This divine experience cannot be engendered by human ingenuity, supersalesmanship, or oratory.

Without the Spirit the world holds a glitter that remains an idle and false hope and appeals to inordinate desires. With the Spirit people have a challenge for joy in the world, a joy that is possible in the measure that they accept the terms of their calling in Christ.

Stewardship — Struggle to Surrender

The victorious struggle in stewardship means fruitfulness. Rachel Henderlite says: "Christ did not die in order that we might live irresponsibly; He died in order that we may live wholly, creatively, as He Himself lived. Our death is necessary in order that Christ may live in us. We must die to ourselves in order that we may live in Him. . . . We who have been long in the church are inclined to take our redemption too lightly. We forget that we cannot go on being slaves when we have once been set free. We hang on to our commonness, forgetting that we have been made holy. We are not willing to leave our transgressions when the Judge has declared us righteous. We want our resurrection without the necessity of being crucified." [6]

Unrepented sins and sinful habits will hinder the stewardship life. The Bible shows us that forgiveness and giving go together. "Therefore, if thou bring thy gift to the altar and there rememberest that thy brother hath ought against thee, leave there thy gift before the altar and go thy way; first be reconciled to thy brother, and then come and offer thy gift" (Matt. 5:23,24). "For Thou desirest not sacrifice; else would I give it; Thou delightest not in burnt offering. The sacrifices of God are a broken spirit; a broken and a contrite heart, O God, Thou wilt not despise" (Ps. 51:16,17). Presenting a contrite and repentant heart should be the first act of Christian stewardship. Sins for which there is no repentance, sins that are excused and rationalized, will stand as a huge wall between the Christian and the dedicated stewardship life.

The writer of Hebrews warns: "Let us lay aside every weight and the sin which doth so easily beset us, and let us run with patience the race that is set before us" (Heb. 12:1). The race is the Christian life, the sanctified life. The reason for faltering steps are the "weights" that hold men down. The contender who is not stripped of impediments is hampered by those weights: the concerns, the selfish interests, and the habitual sins which he is loathe to leave behind. His weakly sanctified life and crawling pace are evidence that he is not facing the sins that plague him nor battling them. Unbridled sin has its own hidden law of gravitation that at every stage pulls its victim a little farther downward. Being so weighted down, the victim cannot run; he cannot walk; he can barely crawl.

After frequent defeats the willpower to resist is gone. The sentries of conscience that stand at the dividing line of right and wrong have been pushed aside and some very dangerous spots are being crossed. Thus the sanctified life becomes gradually weaker. The victim consoles himself with the unquestionable fact that "*all* are sinners," and in his mind all seems right again. According to both Scripture and the Confessions, faith and continuance in unrepented sins are irreconcilable. It is impossible to do as the rich young man tried to do: serve God and money at the same time. The Lord will not tolerate any idol alongside Himself. The idolatry of the works of the flesh (Gal. 5:19-21) must cease, or else faith will falter and finally cease.

What are some of these "weights" or habitual sins? They are sins of the tongue (cursing and gossiping), covetousness and greed. They are fear and doubt, for since they show distrust of God, they surely are terrible, besetting sins. These weights are self-centeredness, material-mindedness, dishonesty, prejudice, lovelessness, self-righteousness, and pharisaism. From all who persist in these sins God calls for a contrite and broken heart (Ps. 51). No matter how pet sins may be explained away, no matter how people will excuse themselves for their outbursts of the flesh, such sins are a distinct hindrance and roadblock to faithful discipleship. "If a man therefore purge himself from these, he shall be a vessel unto honor, sanctified and meet for the Master's use and prepared unto every good work." (2 Tim. 2:21)

The stewardship message, communicating relevant words about sin and grace, should encourage all members to place the big offering on the Lord's altar: the truly repentant heart. For some it may be more important at the moment that they first repent of wicked words that come from their mouths and of the lovelessness in their hearts and of the little "hates" in their lives and then repent of budget shortages in their church. Psalm 51 should be kept fresh in our minds every day and in every stewardship task. Every time we talk improvement, we must also talk repentance.

God's plan for the Christian cleanses and molds and then uses him for His service. The process consists of repentance and forgiveness and faith and then good works. As a result babes become men and women in Christ; it means that the immature become mature; it means that confirmed lives become transformed lives. The covenant plan unites having and hoping for, present sanctification and eschatological fulfillment on the basis of justifying faith.

Repentance, once a word that sounded old-fashioned, is now as up-to-date as the morning newspaper! And the directions of faith are as fresh as the latest worship service, family devotion, and personal meditation.

Desires, once running wild, are now directed to serve life to God's glory; bodies, once temples dedicated to self, now become living sacrifices; tempers, once inclined to glow red hot, now tend to be calm and cool; gossip that hurt others is dropped for words that testify of a merciful Christ; and the incredible smallness of life is left behind for growth in Christ.

Notes for Chapter 2

[1] Charles Malik, "The Gospel and the Life of the Spirit," *The Christian Century*, Aug. 23, 1961, pp. 1001, 1002.

[2] Rachel Henderlite, *Forgiveness and Hope* (Richmond: John Knox Press, 1961), p. 60.

[3] Theodore Heimarck, *Preaching for Tethered Man* (Minneapolis: Augsburg Publishing House, 1962), p. 168.

[4] Gustav Wingren, *Luther on Vocation*, trans. C. C. Rasmussen (Philadelphia: Muhlenberg Press, 1957), p. 68.

[5] T. A. Kantonen, *A Theology for Christian Stewardship* (Philadelphia: Muhlenberg Press, 1956), p. 102.

[6] Rachel Henderlite, *A Call to Faith* (Richmond: John Knox Press, 1955), p. 95.

Chapter 3

The Stewardship Plan

The stewardship struggle continues, but God is not content to watch the struggle as a box seat holder at an athletic affair. God is in our struggle, because He has a plan in which He has involved us.

A truly Biblical stewardship concept will direct members to the fulfillment of God's plan for them. From the Word, R. R. Caemmerer says, the Christian is to be shown "a plan that God has for him, God's judgment on his progress or failure in meeting the plan, and God's grace in Christ by which he is enabled to fulfill the plan." [1]

The Christian Call and Covenant

Believers are "God's picked representatives" and as such God has a plan for each of them and for the body of which they are a part. As God once picked Abraham and told him: "I will bless thee . . . and thou shalt be a blessing" (Gen. 12:2), so He has given Christians His love and mercy by a new covenant to minister to others in His name. As Abraham received God's promises, so Christians through Christ inherit God's gifts to His people (Gal. 3:14,29). As He once took wanderers of the Old Testament and made them His people, so He has taken all believers in Christ, though by nature sinful and obstinate, to be His witnesses and partners to bring the message of pardon and peace to all sinners.

The New Testament shows that the church of Jesus Christ is a spiritual community in and through which God is working out His plan for reaching all men with His love. Believers are "called ones" and "sent ones" who have found that the meaning of all existence was changed when God in His mercy made them participants of His grace through Christ for reaching other people with love. "But you are a chosen race, a royal priesthood, a holy nation, God's own people, that you may declare the wonderful deeds of Him who called you out of darkness into His marvelous light" (1 Peter 2:9 RSV). "You shall be to Me a kingdom of priests and a holy nation" (Ex. 19:6 RSV). "You shall be called the priests of the Lord, men shall speak of you as the ministers of our God." (Is. 61:6 RSV)

We are called to be His people, His appointed ministers in the affairs of His world. In His redemptive grace God singled out a people who are to be His ministers and witnesses. God has cleansed us, called us to faith, and made us a royal people filling royal positions and called by His royal name. He has given us the role to *go to God for people* as we plead for ourselves, our loved ones, our friends and neighbors, and the entire world. We are also commissioned to *go to people for God* as we minister to the needs of all men.

Our priestly functions include the following: "By Him, therefore, let us offer the sacrifice of praise to God continually, that is, the fruit of our lips, giving thanks to His name" (Heb. 13:15). "Let us therefore come boldly unto the throne of grace, that we may obtain mercy and find grace to help in time of need" (Heb. 4:16). "But to do good and to communicate forget not, for with such sacrifices God is well pleased" (Heb. 13:16). "I beseech you therefore, brethren, by the mercies of God, that ye present your bodies a living sacrifice, holy, acceptable unto God, which is your reasonable service" (Rom. 12:1). "I therefore, the prisoner of the Lord, beseech you that ye walk worthy of the vocation wherewith ye are called." (Eph. 4:1)

Through faith we are the new Israel, God's children of promise. This Paul sets forth in his epistles in such passages as the following: "The promise to Abraham and his descendants, that they should inherit the world, did not come through the Law but through the righteousness of faith" (Rom. 4:13 RSV). "So then, they which be of faith are blessed with faithful Abraham" (Gal. 3:9). "Being justified by His grace, we should be made heirs according to the hope of eternal life." (Titus 3:7)

As we accept the covenant of grace, we live by the blessings of God (Rom. 4:16; Gal. 3:14). We both receive and are a blessing — and that is stewardship. Stewardship sends us on a mission to be a blessing to many people. Through God's promise Christ makes His way among us with life-giving power, conquering fear, and makes us living and powerful witnesses to His life, death, and resurrection.

These divine promises are ours: "But my God shall supply all your need according to His riches in glory by Christ Jesus" (Phil. 4:19). "His divine power has granted to us all things that pertain to life and godliness, through the knowledge of Him who called us to His own glory and excellence, by which He has granted to us His precious and very great promises, that through these you may escape from the corruption that is in the world because of passion, and become partakers of the divine nature." (2 Peter 1:3,4 RSV)

God makes the agreement with us, and this covenant which originates in and through God's redemptive act is a relationship that we cannot change or alter, for it rests alone on God's eternal grace. The covenant always implies an offer which God, prompted by His love, makes *to us*.

The call is an act of God's grace in which Jesus takes the initiative. In showing that the words of Jesus in John 15:16, "You did not choose Me, but I chose you, and chose you to bear fruit," could stand as a caption over every story of the calling of disciples, Martin H. Franzmann writes: "Calling is really a divine act. God called Abraham; He called Israel — 'Out of Egypt I called My son' (Hos. 11:1); God called Moses; God called the prophets. Jesus in calling men in this same decisive and exclusive sense is exercising a divine function and prerogative. And so His call . . . is a laying-claim to man. The four who were first called were expected to obey . . . and that 'immediately' and implicitly. . . . To the candidate for discipleship who wanted to go home and first bury his father Jesus made clear the rigor of the renunciation which He demanded by replying, 'Leave the dead to bury their dead' (Matt. 8:22). . . . The renunciation involved in the response of Jesus' creative call is therefore no leap into the dark with eyes closed and teeth clenched. It is a leap into the arms of the Father who clothes the lilies and feeds the birds." [2]

In stewardship activities we as God's "people of promise" are first concerned with the question, "What has God done for us to fulfill the Christian calling?" Only then are we concerned with the question, "What can we do for God?" What we will do for God depends upon what God has already done for us. Thus stewardship efforts and church "loyalty programs" ought to concern themselves more with the fact that God's faithfulness to His promises is the only assurance of our faithfulness to God. The "giving potential" of God is at stake more than ours. Our commitment flows from the fact of God's commitment; first God's faithfulness, then our faithfulness.

Our response in the plan always depends on God's gifts to us. We always take before we can give. Some ask: "Do we have to give up this or that to be a good Christian? Must we give so many hours of service and a certain part of our income in order to be good stewards?" In reality, we *take* from God the gift or grace of generosity, the strength to do without something, and the power of self-discipline. We receive these gifts by promise. In that sense we Christians are always taking, not giving — taking all that God gives and that includes the grace of giving. Some people appear to be unprepared for giving because they have not accepted the grace of giving as children of promise.

Natural man expects to get evidences first, and then go out. God's covenant people do the exact opposite. As Abraham went out, "not knowing where he went," so we perform God's tasks in the faith that He will bless and prosper us.

The task is attached to a promise. If we will do what we can, God will do what we cannot do. For God deals with His people *not in terms of demand but of promise.* God does not seek something *from* His people as much as something *for* them. This speaks volumes for the conduct of stewardship programs: they do not have the authority of demands, but the responsibility of sending people out *with promise.* As God's people we are a holy people, a covenant nation, a servant people, His body.

The Covenant Plan in Daily Life

The *whole* church is now the priesthood. The clergy of the church do not have an essentially different status from that of the layman. The difference is one of office and type of service given. The Christian vocation or priesthood means this: God called the believer in Christ; then He put him into a calling or vocation; in the Christian vocation (and more specifically his occupation) he is to be a "calling one."

God's call does not take the Christian out of the world but leaves him in it with definite functions. It is through all its members that the church makes some of the most significant contacts in daily life. The business of God's adopted children is to represent Him and to share His love in their relationship to all people of every class, tongue, and race. Projecting the love of God to all the people we meet, our lives should be a demonstration of what God can do with human clay. We are not only to tell the Good News of God to others, but also to protest every betrayal of the Savior and His Word. We dare not by unconcern or inactivity abdicate our positions of witness or hand over society and business to the leadership of non-Christians.

Faithful stewardship lives can be observed by providing the Word of Christ in such ways as a mother teaching her children the Sunday school lesson, a father conducting the family devotion, a child studying the school lessons well, a neighbor showing love toward an unfortunate family, a workingman giving honest labor every day, a homemaker showing a pleasant attitude in all her work in the home, a couple planning together their home which is to be built on Christ, a loyal citizen taking interest in and working for his government and for his political party to make it as positive and as helpful as possible, a businessman wisely investing his earnings in a God-pleasing manner, a church member working on a committee or in an organization to advance the Kingdom, a family showing kindness and tenderness toward those who experience violence and inequalities, and the shut-in's fervent prayer for the Spirit's blessings upon all those priests in their many positions of witness in the world.

A distinguished theologian told a gathering of laymen: "Our assembled, corporate worship is, so to speak, rehearsal. Here on Sunday at 11 o'clock we worship God in a practice session among ourselves in order that we may more skillfully worship Him the rest of the week dispersed among other people. The rest of the week it is our ministry to adore Him and intercede for the world in the midst of the world." [3]

The life of the church is not what takes place only on Sunday morning, and stewardship is not only what is done in church programs. More "pew sitters" can be gained without getting the church more into the world. The church is not brought out of the world for one morning a week in the hope of sterilizing the members for another week of contamination in the world. The goal is not to gain recruits for church services, but to gain recruits for the total ministry of the church of Jesus Christ. The church's major arena of activity or battlefront is not in its committees and conferences, but in the common life of all Christians in their homes, in the stores, in their government, and in their total lives.

We have an ambassadorship that covers the social, political, and economic areas of our lives. The Scriptures do not teach that church tasks are sacred while everyday secular tasks are nonsacred. Rather, we have an all-embracing purpose for our lives, a unity of the spiritual and the material. This means service to ourselves and to others in spiritual, physical, intellectual, and social concerns.

The Covenant Plan in the Organized Church

In practice, congregations have tended to limit the Christian vocation to what happens in the church building or church program. The merely institutional and organizational understanding of the universal priesthood and the Christian vocation is harmful. The congregation can ill afford to "use" (the term usually employed) laymen only to feed the organization, as it has often done; it must aim to equip them for their work of a fully functioning ministry. (Eph. 4:12)

When a false distinction is made between "full-time" Christian workers and those believers who find their calling in business, professional life, and other services, the Christian vocation has been distorted. The embodiment of the church in the world is the ministering laity. Proper stewardship emphases seek to implement this sacred plan.

It is possible to be considered "successful" church workers and as having "successful" church programs without being relevant communicators of the Word of God — without being serious about the crucial issues of the people's true priestly functions. There is a somewhat deceptive religious front in today's society that has also marked some of the activity of the church. There are impressive new buildings, growing congregations, popular programs, larger budgets, and plenty of publicity. Amidst this the church has been developing growing leadership and maturing Christians. Yet behind a facade of religion many homes are disintegrating and love of money is becoming more passionate, and people are tormented by more fears. Many have the notion that Christians may carry on their church activities while keeping their shameful prejudices and habitual sins.

We have a deepening conviction that most deficiencies in church work can be traced to a failure to follow adequately the doctrine of Christian vocation and the priesthood of all believers. Too many messages and methods come as disjointed efforts to meet some emergency and immediate need, and there is some disparity between present-day church life and what the New Testament presents. The concern should be for the spiritual fulfillment of individuals, not simply for loyalty to traditions or the organization.

There are those who really do not understand the practical meaning of the Christian calling and the priestly function of all believers. There are also those who understand it but do not put it into practice because too many other matters take their time for sufficient thinking and planning. Some who really believe they are encouraging members towards the fulness of the call actually are not. Small successes in church work have tended to help some groups settle back and rest on little laurels already won. Stewardship emphases should have a spontaneous, built-in, spiritual quality, a "servant-consciousness" that sees every Christian ministering to the world with all his gifts in every way possible.

Stewardship Based on the Call and Covenant

Christian stewardship finds its deepest meaning and strongest theological base in the Christian vocation and the priesthood of all believers. This call to be God's people constantly reminds us of God's active and gracious purpose for the world. As the theology of stewardship grows out of the covenant and Christian vocation, it deepens the dimensions of stewardship to a constant call to repentance and faith.

The traditional term of a "householder" does not have the fulness and dynamic meaning for the stewardship of life embodied in the concept of Christian vocation within the covenant. The householder concept speaks of Christians under the vigilance and even the condemnation of the owner, and it invites threat and Law because it contains no inherent Gospel. Even though there are strong Gospel overtones in the "householder" concept, the Gospel must be imported to it, and that causes some real difficulties. Except for Paul's use of stewardship in his letters to the Corinthians, it is used mostly in the context of judgment.

The householder references of the Bible encourage shrewdness in use of means, but do not show the basis of stewardship; they show "how to" but do not contain inherently all the factors of "why." We believe the householder metaphor is a very worthy term to employ to indicate how man may respond, but it is not broad enough for portraying the fulness of response in the covenant relation. The use of this term by the church has been too limiting. The modern church has tended to take the term out of its theological context and has therefore failed to realize the fullest meaning of stewardship.[4] We believe that the theological concept of stewardship grows out of the great covenant theme of sonship and the Christian calling which inherently conveys grace and power.

Basing the concept of stewardship upon the Christian's vocation or calling, we ask: "Who is calling? Who is called? How is he called? On what terms is he called? For what purpose is he called? How is the call fulfilled and carried out?" These questions encompass the deepest meaning of the entire Christian life and find a wholeness and unity that puts all stewardship into proper focus. This concept is the stewardship key by which Christians can know their mission in the world as the people of God. The Christian vocation suggests the right questions and provides the right answers for Christian stewardship. And it properly projects into view the place of the Word, message, method, and all the other parts that make for an effective stewardship emphasis.

God's plan says that as each believer listens to the Gospel his life becomes a response to that Gospel. His life becomes a dialog with others as a servant of this Word. The Christian calling proceeds from the immeasurable worth of every individual before God to the special concern and care that God wants to give each individual. The proclamation of mercy does not go out from God to mankind in general only, but it also proceeds specifically from person to person in the ministration of His Word.

For practical purposes we will use interchangeably the terms priesthood, the people of God, the Christian vocation and calling. These will serve as the metaphors for the stewardship base, for a steward is a priest — and a priest is a steward.[5]

Notes for Chapter 3

[1] R. R. Caemmerer, *Preaching for the Church* (St. Louis: Concordia Publishing House, 1959), p. 15.

[2] Martin H. Franzmann, *FOLLOW ME: Discipleship According to St. Matthew* (St. Louis: Concordia Publishing House, 1961), pp. 5, 6.

[3] Robert E. Huldschiner, "The Lay Perversion of the Church," *The Lutheran Quarterly*, XIV, No. 3 (August 1962), 218.

[4] Helge Brattgard in his outstanding stewardship study entitled *God's Stewards* (Minneapolis: Augsburg, 1963) develops the "householder" concept in an excellent manner.

[5] Books on the Christian vocation which stewardship leaders should find helpful for personal growth and for resource material are: Richard R. Caemmerer, *God's Great Plan for You* (St. Louis: Concordia Publishing House, 1961); Donald R. Heiges, *The Christian Calling* (Philadelphia: Muhlenberg Press, 1958); Frances O. Ayers, *The Ministry of the Laity* (Philadelphia: Westminster Press, 1962); Elton Trueblood, *The Company of the Committed* (New York: Harper & Brothers, 1961). The author has supplied a filmstrip (*Me in a Pulpit?*), a book (*Your Pulpit in Life*), and a flipchart ("You and Your Pulpit") as an educational package to aid a congregation in conducting an EMV or a 6-week orientation program on the priesthood of all believers. (St. Louis: Church-Craft Pictures, 1962)

Chapter 4

Stewardship Motivations

Under the covenant call the plan for stewardship is clear. We may understand the plan and know it, but certain voices tempt us to forget it and try something else. We can be distracted from it by modern methods of promotion and propaganda, and by emphasis on money, debts, and various pressures that endanger our consciousness that we are the called people of God under His covenant of grace. When this purpose of God is forgotten, wrong motivations follow.

The failure to understand properly the motives of God's plan for the redeemed has resulted historically in some serious stewardship errors and has raised many problems.

The Christian's conduct springs from his theology and his beliefs. "For as he thinketh in his heart, so is he" (Prov. 23:7). We have deep-rooted convictions, and because of these convictions we act the way we do. Our motives are many and complex.

Christians can easily be confused when improper or sub-Christian motives are suggested to them for performing various stewardship tasks. F. B. Edge points out: "This is a fundamental problem. If people are busily engaged in carrying out many different acts which are related to the church but which have little or no Christian foundation or motivation, by such 'busyness' we are leading them to deceive themselves into thinking that they are something they are not . . . this is not theological hair-splitting. It is a basic issue. It is a fundamental difference between Christianity and modern Pharisaism." [1]

The secularistic and materialistic motives of our society have invaded the church, many of them contradicting the Gospel plan. Secularism has had its effect on motives and behavior. Self-interest has too often passed as a pseudo-Christian ethic or motive. Self-centeredness and self-concern are tyrants and enemies of the Christian life and of the acts of stewardship and giving. Some say, "Every good guy gives!" Thus popular stewardship is molded to fit the capacities of the unconverted and is preoccupied with gaining fruit by appealing to the unregenerate attitudes of mankind. Some motives that may be acceptable for public fund drives would seem like bribes within the church. If "every good guy gives," then his gift is proof that he is a good guy. But does a gift of five or ten dollars make him a "good guy"?

Examples of false motives that violate the covenant plan in Christian stewardship and giving may be found among the following:

1. An appeal to a sense of duty. "You belong to the church, so it's your duty to support it," the canvasser may argue. In a sense it is the Christian's duty, but that is not a motive to which we appeal. The Christian's real reason for giving can be found in the nature and terms of the covenant with God.

2. An appeal to pride. "You can't give more to the church than the poor widow down the street?" asks the canvasser. "First Church has never missed its benevolence and mission budget. If we don't get more generous gifts in December, we will miss it for the first time." This reason for raising sufficient mission offerings wrongfully appeals to the member's pride. Possibly First Church deserves to miss its goal so that its leaders may be led to reflect on their motives and messages.

3. An appeal to personal loyalty to the minister, personal taste for a church building, or for certain traditional church activities. These are often based on sympathy for a particular

personality or a favorite activity. When leaders try to cash in on the popularity of their pastor or of some project to gain their ends, they have perverted the Gospel motive.

4. An appeal to give more generously because "we have never had it so good." When such a reason is pressed upon people, it will backfire in the end and often result in stunted stewardship activity. If leaders remind people of their full bank accounts during prosperity (as a motive to give more), then in lean years leaders will be reminded by members of their empty bank accounts. To say "The land is fat" as a general appeal is not quite fair because there are always some in the group who find themselves "financially thin" — thus the appeal points to some irrelevant facts and away from the spiritual truths.

5. An appeal to the need of the Christian to give. Neither the need of the Christian to give nor the need of the congregation to receive support is a fundamental Christian motive for giving. This need does exist as a result of our being Christians, but it dare never be stressed as a motive.

6. An appeal to fear. Fearful pleas such as, "This is our last chance," or, "This is a once-in-a-lifetime opportunity" are not expressive of proper motivation for graceful giving. Too many Christians give generously only when they are moved by some powerful appeal to relieve a case of immediate need or to meet an emergency. Why should a high-pressure, emotional appeal be required to move men to do that which should be their normal course of action? Giving should not be regulated by sentiment and impulse but by principles of Scripture and grace.

An appeal to the budget or to the needs of the congregation. Harry G. Coiner writes: "When the funds are not coming in and the budget is not being met in the church, several temptations arise. One is to condemn and exhort the misers by publishing a list of contributions; another is to seek to squeeze out a bigger flow of funds by some new and more clever fund-raising approach. The proper strategy is always to dig deeper and to use the Gospel . . . God's dynamite, to blast open the way to the inexhaustible underground river of God's grace." [2]

When we face people with the stewardship challenge, we must try to understand the complexities of their minds and motives. Even when the message is clear and the mind comprehends the challenge on its own level of understanding and experience, it may be confused because of the set of values the individual has accepted. Many wrong motives demonstrate the complexity of motivation in stewardship. We may urge gifts in pity of the heathen or the poor. Some may point to tax exemptions, which are a blessing but certainly not a motivation. Some want good stewardship practices to build a new world order. Statistics may be used to urge better giving habits.

A study of the possible stewardship motives indicates that great care is needed in the development of stewardship messages and methods lest some false and sub-Christian standards be presented. When congregational stewardship activities are conducted, there is the danger of diverting attention from the real motivations inherent in the Gospel.

Reward and fear of punishment are high in the minds of many people. Yet it seems that Jesus introduced the thought of reward not as an inducement but rather as an encouragement for His followers to persevere in the loyalty and consecration *which they had already shown.* C. F. H. Henry says: "The exclusion of final divine recompense as an element in the contemplation of moral responsibility leads to incomplete and inadequate systems of ethics." [3] The stewardship act is not done because it is profitable but because it is part of God's plan for us.

The expectation of any reward becomes a matter of faith, and the reward itself is a matter of grace. Jesus did often appeal to final enjoyment or pain, but the prospect of pleasure or pain was not presented as the motive for living the Christian life. Our Christian hope allows us to give up earthly security and to cast ourselves trustingly into the hands of God. The Bible clearly teaches that God by grace will pay the justified man according to his deeds, but such teaching does not reduce Christianity to the level of rewards and punishments. Actions are not to be swayed by ulterior considerations. God's grace does not provide a bargain counter. The immediate and final advantages which may result from right conduct are not the motivation, but God's merciful love to mankind is the motive. The deeds of Christianity are not to be charged to ulterior motives or calculated selfishness, for salvation is already ours in Christ; heaven is a "present" hope, so it cannot be a reward.

The theme of grateful love is woven throughout the fabric of the New Testament. Thankfulness is shown by St. Paul to be a part of the Christian life, while thanklessness is indicated as one of the great sins of life. Yet more is involved. If gratitude for material gifts is put forth as a major motive for stewardship, then "we must have a deeper understanding of what gratitude implies," writes Helge Brattgård. "That which is of decisive significance here is to distinguish properly between the Giver and the gifts. Gratitude of a moralistic nature is always bound to the gifts. A person does good because he himself has received good gifts. But if a man's relation to God and his neighbor is determined by the gifts he has received, then he is no longer living in gratitude but in demand. And chances are good that the man who has such an attitude is one who has done well in an earthly sense. . . . Christian theology refers insistently to the fundamental difference between the Giver and the gifts. When a man is living in a right relationship to God, his position before God is independent of the gifts He gives. Such a man is bound to the Giver in faith. This implies that God is permitted to give freely. Man trusts in God Himself, and not in His gifts. Only in such a spirit can we receive what is given in true gratitude born out of confidence in the Giver." [4]

Brattgård suggests that God's love and His living concern

for us are the reasons for gratitude and that our trust is in God's goodness, not in the good things of the material world. This gratitude continues whether we have much or little, whether we are given long-term use of the good things of the world or not. "The fruit does not result from the gratitude of the tree. It rather grows out of the vital connection in which the tree stands to the Creator. Only when a man stands in an unconditional relationship to God, in which he permits God to give and take freely, only then can we receive gifts in confidence and lose them without despair. Only thus can we live a life of true gratitude. And this is possible only in faith." [5]

Gratitude can be easily misunderstood, and it can be used as an easy exhortation. "Be grateful!" can be a wrongful moralistic exhortation. Gratitude is also a grace from God and is to be sought from Him, for it cannot be worked up in ourselves by our own power. Gratitude is not a motivation; gratitude is a response and response takes form in specific acts. Gratitude is a fruit, not a root. In a sense gratitude is not a keynote of stewardship, and it can easily become a general moral consciousness of responsibility. The motive is God's love for man, not man's love for God. Man's love for God comes after God's love has moved man to love.

The motivation is not, "You have failed," but, "Look who you are." The stewardship issue is centered in these statements: "See what God's grace has done and continues to do for you! Behold what manner of love the Father has bestowed upon you! See what your possibilities and opportunities are through your 'in Christness' and by His power and grace! Know God's great plan for you!"

God's Covenant Word Is the Means for Motivation

Stewardship efforts can center too much on men's voices and ideas and thus gain an improper independence from God's Word. God calls leaders and members to confront one another with the Word of God, not with human motivations.

It's a ministry of *God's* Word, not of *man's*. Man's word reaches the *ear* only, but God's Word reaches the *heart*. The majestic and powerful Word stands against men's words. The Word is the point of contact for faith.

God's Word unites men in their tasks. Man's word encourages men to attend to their tasks, but it always has the power to divide them into the "for" and "against" groups. This means that stewardship efforts dare never stay on the level of such exhortations as: "Let us do this . . . let us stop this . . . let us give, give, give . . . the church is asking. . . ." Much more is needed than exhortations based on statistics about worship and Communion attendance, about lack in church treasuries, and about needs of world missions. The key words of stewardship motivation are not "promote" and "support" — not "promote" for the leaders and "support" for the members!

Stewardship will be nothing more than a program contrived by men if it is not made a vehicle for communicating Gospel motivation in a relevant manner. Where excitement is aroused by hair-raising mission stories only, faith will fail; where there is encouragement and inspiration from men only, faith will cease; where there is humanitarian interest only, faith will vanish. Faith that is wrought by the Word and sacrament and undergirded by worship will not be half-hearted; it will not soon fail or pass away.

Nothing is gained by reading the bylaws to members instead of exposing them to the Bible and God's dynamic to achieve greater sanctification. Moral decisions and conflicts in relation to stewardship cannot be worked out morally or by pyschological factors, the solution is found in another dimension, the Word of God itself. There is only a very narrow margin for conversation with members when they are judged according to psychological, moral, or sociological criteria, and by secondary spiritual suppositions which may appear correct in themselves but which the Holy Spirit through the Word makes totally irrelevant. Proclamation is the watchword — not persuasion and salesmanship. The Word will reveal where there is a theological gap in programs, a dichotomy between theology and practice, aspiration and actuality, message and method.

Human nature does not give up even if it daily hears words that challenge its conceptions. The old Adam will listen to man's words, for he wants to hear messages where the scandal of the Word, the sacrifice, and the cross are minimized.

R. Henderlite proposes: "It is the responsibility of the church, then, to open the Bible for its members in such a way that they may come to it in faith, ready to hear God speak and in speaking to lead them into covenant. For the people of God must listen again and again to the story of their life, how God took them when they were no people and made them His people. And as they listen, the event occurs again, and man meets God and is created anew." [6]

There comes a time after the Word of grace has been sown in hearts, watered with care, and the ground carefully cultivated that we must step aside and say: "Dear Lord, we have tried to be faithful in our planting and cultivating. We have given Thy people Thy Word in sermon, in topics, and in our stewardship efforts. We have nourished them with Thy promises. We have pointed to the coming harvest. We ask Thee, dear God, give the increase and make Thy people yield bounteously beyond our fondest expectations. Cause them to respond to Thy great salvation through Thy indwelling Spirit. Let them be the kind of people who will glorify Thee! In Jesus' name." Then we can hopefully say "Amen," go out for a day of fishing and rest, and go to sleep peacefully. The ripening harvest is in good hands — God's hands.

Only God can keep us aware of our calling and opportunities to serve Him. He alone can motivate us for our calling or revive us when we become weary. It is not possible for people to motivate other people, but God gives us His Word, both the judging and the forgiving Word, to call one another to repentance and to renew us for His covenant plan.

The Covenant Word of Judgment and Grace
Directs Us on the Covenant Path

The motivation for stewardship response can never be had apart from knowing the judgment of the Law for our failures and the forgiveness of the Gospel in our service to God. Motivation is provided by recalling people to their Christian vocation of baptismal power and of Holy Communion. The struggles of the covenant life are won and Christian stewardship is made possible through the proclamation of God's judging Word (the Law) which reveals man's sinfulness and through God's forgiving Word (the Gospel) which proclaims God's love and mercy for man's renewal. The stewardship concept must avoid the distortion of either the Law or the Gospel, guarding the former from the perversion of legalism and the latter from antinomianism.[7] Law and Gospel are both messages from God. The Gospel declares the mercy of God, whereas the Law condemns.

Christians are no longer in bondage to a moral law they cannot fulfill, binding their consciences to a plan for life or a scheme of stewardship behavior beyond their reach, or showing them that they are slaves of sin. God's free grace to us has renewed our lives with liberty and assurance.

In the article "The Secret of God's Plan" Coiner tells of God's gracious acts in man's stewardship: "Christian stewardship is an activity which must be understood and accepted in faith as an abiding principle that inheres in the creating, redeeming, and sanctifying activity of a gracious God. God has made us, redeemed, called, renewed, and empowered us to live to the praise of His glory and to carry out His holy purposes to bring salvation to men." [8]

Why is it that we are often "tongue-tied about laying the full gift of God and Christ Jesus plainly before the minds of our people and pressing and rubbing it in?" asks Richard R.

Caemmerer. He replies: "Part of the answer lies in this that we are also terribly afraid to stand up and be counted on what we call the Law, that we are afraid to denounce unbelief and call death death; that we do not quake with terror before the power of an avenging God and are too ineffably tender at causing the man before us to quake with the recognition of who He is and that He is, indeed, a jealous God and that His wrath is evident already in our age against those who have turned away from Him. We are afraid to interpret to people the immediacy, the dreadful immediacy of the fact that God holds us in judgment for our lives, made us for His purposes, and recoils in His wrath over our failure to do His will. The Gospel of God alone is God's answer to this predicament, to this dread death, to this horrible spiritual rigor mortis that besets men here and now. . . . There is no such thing as preaching Gospel [alone]. We always preach Law and Gospel or we do not preach at all, we only make sermons, we only behave ourselves as pleasant men in an apathetic and torpid world. This is a thing, indeed, that we could learn from our Lord Christ, that He could flame in indignation and He could beseech with kindness. We could learn from St. Paul that he could speak of the bewitched Galatians as youngsters whom he had brought to birth, for whom he had been simultaneously mother and midwife at their coming into the world, and whom he could cause to face the curse that had to be laid on those who had misled them." [9]

God's Covenant Word of Judgment: The Law

Because we are flesh and have the old nature, we need to experience the use of the keen-edged sword of discipline and the Law against this old nature. God's Law reveals man's stewardship delinquencies. Karl Kretzschmar says that the well-known passage, "By the Law is the knowledge of sin" (Rom. 3:20), may well be paraphrased thus: "The knowledge of stewardship offenses is by the Law." [10]

When the Law is properly used, it should cut deeply into the flesh. Sin needs to be exposed, and the heart must be bared. This cannot be done by merely verbalizing sin. Our sinner-side refuses to do God's will and so needs to be exposed by the Law. C. F. W. Walther says: "Now, lest the preaching of the Gospel only produce lazy, frigid Christians, who imagine that they need not do good works, the Law says to the old Adam: Sin not; be godly; shun that, do this, etc." [11] The Law must be preached sharply to crucify the old man, not to empower the new man for good works. In this matter Walther shows how the Law may be misused: "There is to be no ranting about abominable vices that may be rampant in the congregation. Continual ranting will prove useless." [12] "Take the sin of avarice. A congregation may be so stingy as to refuse to take up a collection; it may fail to pay the pastor his salary. In that case the pastor must not resolve to preach his people a sharp sermon in order to open their purses. Opening purses by means of the Law is no achievement at all. He must preach in a manner that will rouse them out of their spiritual sleep and death." [13] "Possibly he may increase the collection by a few dollars, but the offering is worthless in the sight of God, because it was made under coercion." [14] "The attempt to induce those who are already believers in Christ to do good by holding up the Law and issuing commands to them is a very gross confounding of Law and Gospel." [15]

The old man cannot escape the condemnation of the Law, and so he always stands under it. The neglect of the Law causes warfare to cease against sin. However, Luther said that the Law may well point the way, but that it is far from being the strength of one's legs. By avoiding the use of the Law, we only add to the measure of our delinquencies and make our position in the final accounting all the more hopeless. Under the Law we are left without comfort or hope for fellowship with God.

The Law is the tutor that takes us to the school of the

Savior to receive His grace. St. Paul says: "Wherefore the Law was our schoolmaster to bring us to Christ, that we might be justified by faith" (Gal. 3:24). The Law is a mirror to reveal to us our true situation. In the Christian life the Law is a guide or suggestion which directs to the will of God. It is important that we understand these Scriptural truths so that we do not become guilty of making the performance of stewardship acts a legal requirement.

Under grace the Law also serves as the criterion of moral good and virtue. Faith takes note of the will of God as revealed in the Law, for it sets forth a guide for us. The Law exposes weaknesses, and then the Gospel leads to freedom of action, personal initiative, resourcefulness, voluntary procedures, the exercise of personal judgment, and the right to make decisions by the power of God.

He who proclaims God's Word must be both demanding and giving in relation to others. At one time he may bring the severity of God's judgment together with the news of God's goodness, while at another time he may bring only the gentleness of the Gospel of forgiveness. Both the will and love of God must be visible in the ministry of stewardship leaders — and of the members. No single pattern can be adequate.

God's Covenant Word of Grace: The Gospel

God motivates as we serve one another by proclaiming His covenant Word of grace. Faithfulness to the call is always the product of the Gospel. Stewardship can have no other foundation than the Gospel of forgiveness. God's absolving and strengthening grace is the theological thread in His plan that keeps all stewardship messages and activities in proper perspective.

The Gospel, not the Law, furnishes the motive power for Christian stewardship. While the Law only causes the Christian to pull his cloak of stubborn resistance and unwillingness more closely about himself, the sun of the Gospel with its penetrating power and warming love induces and enables

55

the steward to pull off his cloak of selfishness and to get to work in the service of his Lord. Man's idolatry must be broken down; the Law reveals this idolatry, but the Gospel is God's way of breaking it down. Melting and activating the heart is the work of the Gospel. Gospel as motivation does not preclude a strong use of the Law to awaken the heart to a desperate need of God's grace for stewardship acts.

When the Gospel is not clearly understood, the merit system of good works comes on the scene. In Galatians St. Paul points out that the error of merit or "good works" has two forms: (1) works have a part in becoming justified; (2) the justified believer attains perfection through good deeds in obedience to the Law. Of the first error St. Paul wrote: "A man is not justified by the works of the Law, but by the faith of Jesus Christ" (Gal. 2:16). Concerning the second, a more subtle form, he pointed to the *union* with Christ and showed that this is the cause of "faith which worketh by love." (Gal. 5:6)

We are free from the Law, but not in order that we may be free to do whatever we please. In fact grace by the Gospel sets a higher challenge. "Therefore be imitators of God, as beloved children. And walk in love, as Christ loved us and gave Himself for us, a fragrant offering and sacrifice to God." (Eph. 5:1,2 RSV)

There ought to be no complaining about a lack of fruit if there is little effective planting of the seed and nourishment by the covenant Word of grace. William Keech shows the gravity of this problem as he writes: "It is no wonder that many are welcoming a new study of stewardship which is rooted not in the psychology of salesmanship but in the Gospel. Many nominal members of the church are not good stewards because their lives are based upon a pattern of convictions that is more secular or pagan than Christian. They do not really believe that their lives, their possessions, their time, their talents, and their associations belong to God." [16]

Grace says that there is nothing man can give that he has

not first received. What is this grace of God? "It means the One who at the same time makes absolute demands upon us offers freely to *give* us all that He demands. It means the One who requires of us unlimited obedience and then supplies the obedience Himself. It means the One who calls us to work out our own salvation on the ground that 'it is He Himself who works both the willing and the working' in our hearts and lives. It is not that He bestows His favour, His grace, upon those who render obedience to His commands. Such divine giving in response to human obedience is a sub-Christian idea, alien to the New Testament; and indeed if God's grace had to wait for man's obedience, it would be kept waiting forever." [17]

The stewardship life is due only to God's grace (Eph. 2:1-10), God's power of "making alive" and "keeping alive" by the Gospel. Without this grace man cannot know supernatural truths nor attain to supernatural things. God's act of love radically reverses man's life and sets him to follow God's plan.

Human Motivations Confuse and Obstruct God's Motivational Plan

We see three *motivational* levels operating in us as we live our Christian lives:

1. *You must* — This is law, lack of freedom, without choice.

2. *You ought to* — This is moral obligation, feeling of duty, moral responsibility, compulsion.

3. *You will want to* — This is grace, freedom, love, spontaneity, recklessness, hilariousness.

St. Paul is obviously very concerned about motivation in the covenant life. His letter to the Romans explains the place of Law in our lives, and this is a guide for its meaning in the stewardship life. St. Paul even rejects compulsion ("not of necessity" — 2 Cor. 9:7 and Philemon 14) *as motivation.* M. H.

57

Grumm suggests: "There is a significant absence of words of obligation in contexts of motivation in Paul's epistles. That the Christian is under a tremendous obligation is a fact to Paul. He feels it strongly. But he does not preach it to motivate to action." [18]

The motivating Gospel changes the tormenting "Thou shalt" and the distressing "I ought" to the "I want to" or to "I will by the grace of God." The stewardship life and morality are no mechanical result of a leader's urging the Law. Grace took us out from under the Law once and forever when Christ took us out, and we must avoid getting under new laws proposed by men.

T. A. Kantonen writes: "The enthusiasms which are drawn from man's emotional resources are soon used up. Weariness and exhaustion set in. The only alternative then left is the legalistic 'You must.' The obstreperous will is flogged with exhortations: 'You must do better,' 'You must try harder.' Sensitive consciences are thus led to despondency, the less sensitive to self-righteousness. With the Gospel of grace the case is entirely different. It is in the indicative, a narrative of what God has done and is doing, not in the imperative, a demand to man to do something." [19]

The Gospel causes us to give; the demands of the Law do not. Note these differences in Christian giving between the demands of the Law and the grace of the Gospel:

1. Law: give and live
   Grace: live and give

2. Law: give with a view to being something
   Grace: makes you something with a view to give

3. Law: saved and kept *by* giving
   Grace: saved and kept *for* giving

4. Law says: "If you will give, I will bless you"
   Grace says: "I have blessed you, and you will be a giver"

58

Leaders are called to guide people into fruitful lives. Let them use the Word of judgment and forgiveness in such a way that Christians will want to express their faith and serve their Lord. Legalistic and psychological devices are to be avoided. It is easy to "clobber" the people, to "ride" them and tell them they must do something solely because it is their "duty" or because God has "commanded" them to do so.

Legalism finds man taking things into his own hands and attempting to force action or fruit by human contrivances or motivations. This is a very big problem in our "success-conscious" age. Activities related to stewardship efforts in some congregations reveal a suspicious though unintended tendency in the direction of legalism and moralism. Stewardship efforts lend themselves to making the Gospel into a new law in order to accomplish current hopes and plans.

The New Testament does not allow the adoption of any type of legalistic system which relieves God's people of the freedom and responsibility of making their own decisions. Life under grace does not allow a codification of activities that are to be performed, but it does expound the possibilities of the bond of sonship in God and of fellowship that exists in Christ.

Carl Henry indicates the serious nature of legalistic measures: "Arbitrary legalism is a poor substitute for an inner morality. . . . Such legalism emphasizes the less-important issues in life, and ignores or excuses the weightier matters. . . . Not only does legalism bypass the sins of the spirit, but it gives the impression that the Christian life is one of staying out of trouble. . . . Christian morality is not just negative abstinence. It is positive virtue flowing out from the regenerated core of the person." [20]

Confusion in motivation is created and the Gospel loses its centrality when artificial and fleshly devices are contrived to get action from people. Pleas of loyalty, cries of emergencies (created because of laxness), and organizational claims have a detrimental effect when used as motivation.

Under such conditions the giving response will not be due primarily to God's Word but to the demands to meet human standards. We must not equate the Gospel with "duty" and the achievement of institutional goals. The Gospel loses its dynamic when it is converted into behavior and habit patterns. Then it has been perverted into law. In this regard there may be more semi-Pelagian and synergistic practices in our midst than we realize — involuntary and inadvertent — but real.[21]

The final moments of the sermon present a great temptation for moralizing, for commingling Law and Gospel, for using the Gospel as a whip to encourage good works. After 20 minutes of Gospel one might be tempted to recall that things are getting worse in the parish (church attendance is worse this summer than last, Bible Class attendance never was good, some people have not been to Communion for nine months, the budget deficit is getting bigger, etc.) — at this moment it may be stated with great indignation: "What's the matter, don't we appreciate the Gospel? The way we are acting, we don't even merit the preaching of the Word and salvation . . . ." People might say after this that the pastor really "laid it on the line today," but they will not be motivated to change.

Rather, the last five minutes of the sermon should allow the minister to show *what God's grace will do for the member today* (he has just been shown what God's grace has done for him in the past); he is shown the power of God that will make the weakest one strong to do that which one would normally shy away from; he is shown the Gospel melting the coldest heart, including his.

In his epistle St. Paul shows how to apply the Gospel as encouragement for the sanctified life. He says: "I beseech . . . *by the mercies of God* (what a resource!) . . . present your bodies a living sacrifice . . . be not conformed to this world . . . but be ye transformed . . . I say, *through the grace given unto me*" (Rom. 12:1-3). He urges: "Your body is the *temple of the Holy Ghost . . .* bought with a price; there-

60

fore glorify God in your body"(1 Cor. 6:19,20). He beseeches: "We are His workmanship, *created in Christ Jesus* unto good works. . . . able to do exceeding abundantly above all that we ask or think, *according to the power that worketh in us.* . . . beseech you that ye walk worthy of the vocation *wherewith ye are called*" (Eph. 2:10; 3:20; 4:1). He tells: "Stand fast *in* [not *with,* but *in!*] the Lord" (Phil. 4:1). He points out: "If ye then be *risen with Christ,* seek those things which are above, where Christ sitteth on the right hand of God. Set your affection on things above. . . . Christ *is our life.* . . . Put on therefore, *as the elect of God.* . . . Let the Word of Christ dwell *in* you richly. . . . do all in the name of the Lord Jesus" (Col. 3). He shows the goal: "This is the will of God, *even your sanctification*" (1 Thess. 4:3). He reminds: "I beseech you . . . by the coming of our Lord Jesus." (2 Thess. 2:1)

The true Christian life is a living commentary on St. Paul's "therefores." This word usually marks the transition from the telling of God's redemptive act to the living of the life of active stewardship. All the exhortations of the epistles are addressed to those who are baptized, to the regenerate ones, to the new man, to the CHRIST-ian.

Adolf Koeberle says: "The New Testament commands are always preceded by the clear statement of some divine action . . . to show whence the strength for the action comes. All the great deeds of God are enumerated, not in order that they might be supplanted or completed by human actions, but as finished and completed realities that are the basis of faith. . . . The commandment 'Thou shalt have no other Gods before Me' is preceded by the miracle of deliverance. . . . The obligation to fight the good fight of faith, to serve in love, to sacrifice, exists because 'we have such promises' and because we 'are called to eternal life.' Because Christ has taken hold upon us we are already partakers of His resurrection, and for this reason the call comes to us to awaken the gift of God that is in us. . . . To the burning question as to whether sanctification, growth, and constancy are actually possible here on earth there is hardly a clearer answer than the New Testament imperatives that are spoken to congregations existing in a corrupt and perishing world." [22]

Milo Kaufman develops this thought a step further when he writes: "Stewardship of possessions is the effect of God's saving grace upon one's self and his property. . . . When God gets a man with a car He gets a car to be used in His service. . . . Some seem to think of stewardship as a whip or as legal action to drive people to give to the expenses of the church. No doubt too often the attempt has been made to wring generous offerings from selfish souls. Christian stewardship most certainly is not church legislation nor a scheme to deprive men of their cash. It is the natural consequence of an experience with God — the natural reaction of the human heart that has been touched by the divine Spirit." [23]

Notes for Chapter 4

[1] F. B. Edge, *A Quest for Vitality in Religion* (Nashville: Broadman Press, 1963), pp. 152, 153.

[2] Harry G. Coiner, "The Secret of God's Plan," *Concordia Theological Monthly*, XXXIV, No. 5 (May 1963), 274.

[3] C. F. H. Henry, *Christian Personal Ethics* (Grand Rapids: Wm. B. Eerdmans Publishing Co., 1957), p. 546.

[4] Helge Brattgard, *God's Stewards*, trans. Gene Lund (Minneapolis: Augsburg, 1963), p. 150.

[5] Brattgard, pp. 150, 151.

[6] Rachel Henderlite, *Forgiveness and Hope* (Richmond: John Knox Press, 1961), p. 40.

[7] Antinomianism — "anti-law": A controversy during Luther's day in which certain theologians held that the Law has no place in the church because the knowledge of sin, repentance, and the Christian life are derived from the Gospel alone. "The *Formula of Concord* settled the matter by recognizing the triple use of the Law: (1) for outward decency, (2) for revealing sin, (3) for the rule of life to the regenerate, who need it on account of their old Adam." *Concordia Cyclopedia* (St. Louis: Concordia Publishing House, 1927), p. 28.

[8] Coiner, p. 271.

[9] Richard R. Caemmerer, "Friend and Fighter," *Concordia Theological Monthly*, XXXIV, No. 10 (Oct. 1963), 581, 582.

[10] Karl Kretzschmar, *The Stewardship Life* (St. Louis: Concordia Publishing House, 1929), p. 63.

[11] C. F. W. Walther, *The Proper Distinction Between Law and Gospel*, trans. W. H. T. Dau (St. Louis: Concordia Publishing House, 1929), p. 24. This precious gem is a classic which every pastor should find beneficial for frequent reading.

[12] Walther, p. 81.

[13] Walther, p. 303.

[14] Walther, p. 387.

[15] Walther, p. 381.

[16] William J. Keech, *The Life I Owe* (Valley Forge: Judson Press, 1963), p. 43.

[17] D. M. Baillie, *God Was in Christ* (London: Faber and Faber Ltd., 1961), p. 121.

[18] M. H. Grumm, "Motivation in Paul's Epistles," *Concordia Theological Monthly*, XXXV, No. 4 (April 1964), 211.

[19] T. A. Kantonen, *Resurgence of the Gospel* (Philadelphia: Muhlenberg Press, 1948), p. 214.

[20] Henry, p. 421.

[21] The *Pelagian* Controversy took its name from Pelagius (ca. A.D. 400) who taught in essence that man can work out his salvation and righteousness by his own works. Semi-Pelagians later held that salvation depended on grace *and* works.

[22] Adolf Koeberle, *The Quest for Holiness* (Minneapolis: Augsburg Publishing House, 1938), pp. 151, 152. This scholarly volume is a worthy treatment of justification and sanctification — and their relation to each other.

[23] Milo Kauffman, *The Challenge of Christian Stewardship* (Scottdale, Pa.: Herald Press, 1955), pp. 3, 5.

Chapter 5

The Ministry of Personal Stewardship

Stewardship is a personal matter. Each one of us has a personal ministry to be lived to the fullest under the vocation of God in personal discipleship. This ministry of personal stewardship has many facets developed from the deepest meaning of lives rooted in Christ.

The rich variety of images in the Gospels and Epistles helps illuminate the stewardship understanding of God's plan. Personal application of the plan can be seen in our willingness to be servants in the world, in our use of abilities, in our attitude toward our possessions, in our financial investments for the Kingdom, and in our freedom to arrange and order life in response to God's gracious call in the Gospel covenant.

The "Servant" Nature of God's Plan

The plan of God in personal stewardship might best be defined as the "servant" life. The quality of Christian life in the world and in the church is derived from the members' Head, and that quality is "servant" in nature.

Christ not only spoke about the historic redeeming act of God, but He also performed it. The Suffering Servant pictured in Isaiah 53 established a new covenant with men through His blood, which paid the purchase price for the sins of all people. This great fact is told in classic terms in Phil. 2:4-11: "Look not every man on his own things but every man also on the things of others. Let this mind be in you, which was also in Christ Jesus, who, being in the form of God, thought it not robbery to be equal with God, but made Himself of no reputation, and took upon Him the form of a servant, and was made in the likeness of men. And being

65

found in fashion as a man, He humbled Himself and became obedient unto death, even the death of the cross. Wherefore God also hath highly exalted Him and given Him a name which is above every name, that at the name of Jesus every knee should bow of things in heaven and things in earth and things under the earth, and that every tongue should confess that Jesus Christ is Lord, to the glory of God the Father."

"Let this mind be in you, which was also in Christ Jesus!" Christ's words cut across the self-made barriers built by arrogance, covetousness, jealousy, and prejudice. These words allow no mere intellectual approach to life's opportunities and problems. The Amplified New Testament translates this verse: "Let this same *attitude* and *purpose* and *humble mind* be in you." Christ gives Himself to, shares His mind with, and puts His Spirit into those who accept Him in faith. Christ, the Head, is Servant to all, and believers are members of His serving body, the church. "Whoever would be great among you must be your servant, and whoever would be first among you must be slave of all. For the Son of man also came not to be served but to serve and to give His life as a ransom for many." (Mark 10:43-45 RSV)

Christ told the story of the Prodigal Son, and the story gives the clear impression that the father was more interested in having a son than in having a slave. The servanthood must be seen as sonship, not slavery. The servant relationship does not originate with man's duty but with God's love. "Owe no one anything but love" is its theme. Taking the form of a servant is a voluntary act of a son — the Son of Man sets the stage for the redeemed sons of men, who offer the highest service to God and men. "These men are the servants of the most high God, which show unto us the way of salvation." (Acts 16:17)

Christ, the Suffering Servant, heals both the wounds of sin and of bodily suffering. Central to His role is the forgiveness He offers. When the paralytic man was brought to Him for

66

healing (Matt. 9:1-8), Christ said: "My son, your sins are forgiven you." When questioned, He showed how His ministry of healing ("Rise, take up your bed and walk!") centered in His ministry of reconciliation and forgiveness ("Your sins are forgiven").

Whoever serves another creature or creation is enslaved and mastered by someone or something that will pull him farther and farther away from fellowship with God. And a man who is out of fellowship with God is a man out of place. Man is deluded when he goes his own way, for soon he will be enslaved by an environment he was to master.

"If any man come to Me and hate not his father and mother and wife and children and brethren and sisters, yea, *and his own life also,* he cannot be My disciple" (Luke 14:26). A Tokyo businessman who had been a Christian only a few months pointed his finger at this portion of Scripture and said: "These are hard words!" He discovered that Jesus did not want just followers but disciples or servants. Yet Jesus does not ask us to neglect our families but to readjust our relationships and our priorities and to put Him first. No proper human relationship really suffers when Christ is in first place. God does not pit the physical life against the spiritual life, but the spiritual affects the use of the physical and material. When priorities are right, Christian activities and stewardship acts are a joyful expression of faith and not a burden. The dimension of personal stewardship to be sought for the affluent life should not be, "Now that we have it, abandon it," but, "Now that we have it, use it for the purpose God has given it!"

As God in His Son served man's deepest needs, so our stewardship lives are to be shaped to serve other people's needs. Genuine love does not ignore humanity in its great misery. True Christian love discovers and knows that the neighbor exists. To receive God's love is to be set aflame with that same love for the ministry or stewardship He gave us. The function of the body is to make its members available to one another and to their Head, Jesus Christ, and through Him to all mankind.

The servant life is portrayed again in John 12:24,25 (RSV): "Unless a grain of wheat falls into the earth and dies, it remains alone; but if it dies, it bears much fruit. He who loves his life loses it, and he who hates his life in this world will keep it for life eternal." Mark 8:31-38 also presents this picture. This is heaven's own stewardship program, the very principle of life. Spiritual suicide is imminent when one barricades himself in his own little kingdom. When Christ is on the throne, self is put on the cross. The axe of the Word must be put to the very root of the tree of self.

The life imparted to us is a crucified life, a life of death to self and its many masks and forms. The more fully the Crucified One possesses us, the more fully self becomes crucified. As servants of Christ we are living sacrifices for God. "Present your bodies a living sacrifice" (Rom. 12:1). In the Old Testament sacrifices were placed upon the altar to be burned and consumed. In the New Testament the believer himself is the sacrifice. The more we sacrifice of ourselves, the more alive we become. The more we and our will are sacrificed, the stronger we become for service. Our faith will direct all our decisions and will affect our habits of eating, sleeping, and drinking, and faith will suggest answers to indulgences in smoking and other habits too. When we are sacrificed, we will sacrifice many of the false and fleeting fashions of the world. When conversion has taken place, we have really died to ourselves, to our own opinions, tastes, preferences, and will; we have died to the world — its approval or condemnation; we are concerned about the approval of God.

Bonhoeffer tells of an alternative: "We can of course shake off the burden which is laid upon us, but only find that we have a still heavier burden to carry — a yoke of our own choosing, the yoke of our self." [1]

In practical terms of life itself there is a great difference between God's costly reconciliation and man's good-natured indulgence. God certainly does not despise the physical and the material gifts, for He Himself has made them, but He wants them to be used responsibly and sensibly. Christ accepted and used some of earth's material gifts, but He also denied Himself many of the comforts and pleasures of the world when He became a Servant among men. He refused carnal satisfaction, popular acclaim, prestige, and honor — some of the very things which his fellowmen cherished. He willingly accepted poverty, humiliation, sorrow, and death — things that they sought eagerly to escape. His was a life of giving away what the Father had given Him. And so the disciples were to respond to One who loved them and who showed this love by denying Himself while serving them freely.

Yet our commitment and servant position does not imply earthly impoverishment, mediocrity, or undue suffering. God does sometimes prosper some of His people with exceptional health, fortune, and goods. Love will give insights into the way extraordinary gifts should be used. The calculation of what love requires must take into account the understanding and the resources of the one who loves. Then love drives us to identify ourselves with the needs of others: to stand where they stand.

The manifestation of the servant life in our stewardship practice requires self-discipline, so that the victory of the new man over the old may take place. The essence of this servanthood and self-discipline is when we say "No" to self and "Yes" to God, when His will is substituted for ours. Our servant nature includes not only spiritual but also bodily discipline; this is not contempt for the body but reverence for that which God has prepared to be the temple of His Spirit. What God has sanctified we dare not despise or neglect. The servant life will be choked out because of un-disciplined and unrestrained living.

Helge Brattgård gives some insights into the stewardship of the body: "Only a disciplined body can contribute effectively to the work of the steward. . . . Physical discipline is also useful for much (1 Tim. 4:7 f). Paul could see how necessary it was to discipline, to subdue, the body, lest it become a hindrance to the work of evangelism. . . . Within the church, up to now, we have been quite timid about speaking of this side of the Christian life. . . . Our evangelical freedom which is a necessary shield against all ascetic aberrations must not, on the other hand, be interpreted as freedom from the Biblical teaching about the discipline of the body. . . . But love, it must not be forgotten, is the basic regulating principle, for even if a man gives his body to be burned, no one benefits if this is done without love toward his neighbor (1 Cor. 13:3)." [2]

We have a capacity for something far greater than concern for self, and that capacity is part of the challenge under which we live or die. Some of the unquestioned habits and standards of modern society are at issue. We easily get caught in the trap of our own conflicts, our own desire for security, and our fears and doubts. But the world is sick of uncommitted people. Of all people, Christians ought to be the most committed and disciplined — and true servants. Listen to St. Paul: "I am no shadowboxer; I really fight! I am my body's sternest master, for fear that when I have preached to others I should myself be disqualified." (1 Cor. 9:26,27 Phillips)

We should not have to spend time making up our minds where we stand. We ought to be able to jump straight into the fight. It ought to be as plain as daylight what our servanthood means; yet many muddy the situation and falter in their decision by wishful thinking and unrealistic dreaming about what they would do if only their situation were different. In a day of quick prosperity and giveaway shows, it is not easy to interest a well-fed and well-housed Sunday morning group in a "leave all or leave much behind" type of life. Some will sing about taking up their cross to follow

Jesus but want to get the service over so that they can hurry home for rest or for their favorite recreation spot.

Servanthood suggests that several basic questions be faced: What can we do? What can we do without? What can we do with and for others? When these questions are asked, there may be need for a new inventory of the use of every hour, a sharper classification of what is really worth doing and what is merely time-killing. It may mean breaking old habits and learning new ones. It may mean new hopes, new routines, new schedules, and new faces.

The Use of Our Talents

Every Christian has talents and abilities — and they are not of his own choice. God has specifically assigned or given each person certain abilities to be used in His service. The opportunities for service are to match the ability.

Jesus tells of opportunities for service: "To one He gave five talents, to another two, to another one, to each according to his ability" (Matt. 25:15 RSV). Another time Jesus said: "It is like a man going on a journey, when he leaves home and puts his servants in charge, each with his work, and commands the doorkeeper to be on the watch" (Mark 13:34 RSV). God also suggests: "Think with sober judgment, each according to the measure of faith which God has assigned him. . . . Having gifts that differ according to the grace given to us, let us use them . . . in proportion to our faith" (Rom. 12:3,6 RSV). Again: "But grace was given to each of us according to the measure of Christ's gift." (Eph. 4:7 RSV)

Many talents are given individually or in clusters to Christians for use in the church and in their own groups. Some Christians have not seriously tested their capacity. They go on rather haphazardly trying to fill needs only as they are recognized rather than evaluating their capacity and abilities and then planning their ministry according to God's plan. Therefore, they do not meet their responsibility in their personal stewardship. Others attempt too much as they try to

71

pour a gallon of work into their pint-container lives; they fill jobs others ought to be doing, and they stay at a fever pitch of activity without ever quite helping as they should and never enjoying the pace. We should avoid overloading willing workers. When it seems necessary for a willing person to take on additional tasks, the "overloading" should be temporary and done only when unavoidable.

Repeatedly we need to look at the total church "labor market" and assist everyone in searching out the abilities God has given him. The gifts of service are of a great variety. They involve the use of our material resources — cars, money, homes, clothes, food, and all of creation's goodness; our natural and mental aptitudes — handiwork, art, music, teaching, and office work; also our physical strength and abilities — building improvements, landscaping, athletics, and other such activities. Some of the most vital tasks overlooked by most Christians are the responsibility to visit the sick, feed the hungry, clothe the naked, and help the underprivileged. All talents should be channeled into the proper place of need — suited to time, energy, and abilities available.

Other parts of this book indicate the broad use of abilities and how service to God is given beyond churchly tasks. We indicate the gravity of our obligation to exercise our talents in our occupation, in politics and government, in civic groups and community projects, and in every area of life. When people think of talents, they should not consider only outstanding gifts, such as leadership and administration; ability to be instrumentalists, soloists, and artists; and other such specialized talents. In searching for abilities, both great and small, for use in the church and the world, every Christian asks himself: (1) What are my abilities? (2) How am I using them? (3) Do I have any undeveloped abilities? (4) Do I have any unused abilities?

A more specific application can be made to women, who often feel falsely inferior and yet have so much to offer to their church and the world. Ever since Eve, women have

72

been endowed with a special capacity for sensitivity to the needs of others, for tender love, for self-giving, and for understanding. God places human lives in a woman's hands in a special way. As a married woman she may experience God's creative power in her own body as she bears children, and she will find that tending and training children, washing dishes, and cleaning the house are a high calling from God. Denied this experience, the same creativity expresses itself in her relation with others. Women were made by God with ability to bring a special kind of benediction to life. What Christianity did for women was revolutionary, for no other religion, civilization, or movement granted women what Christianity offers them. It gives women a great ministry to people in the family and consequently to the world. Many opportunities for ministry in the church, which women can and should be performing, are neglected by them. Women help refresh the world through their spiritual insight by actively participating in service beyond the family circle in church and community.

In Our Attitude Toward Our Possessions

Personal stewardship is possible through many avenues by use of our time, abilities, and money. Barriers to the proper management of what God has given for use to fulfill His plan are found in the hardness of our heart and wrong attitudes. One of the attitudes with which we must contend most often is that of coveting and of dissatisfaction with what God has given. This often results in sinful use of what God has given rather than in completing our personal work according to His will. This attitude needs further consideration.

Covetousness permeates our natural state. We are born to care for ourselves, and we do not easily shed the inborn characteristics that drive us on in a relentless search for self-satisfaction. The stewardship message of the Gospel collides head-on with our natural instincts about what is "good" for ourselves. When the New Testament declares that a man must "lose his life to find it," that "it is better to give than to receive," or that we should "seek first the kingdom of God," there is instant rebellion within us.

Unless covetousness and materialism are recognized by us as primary roadblocks to the proper use of our possessions, our income, and generous giving, our efforts to teach the personal stewardship of life will only go through the motions. Unless we are confronted, and confront others, with the wreckage this sin makes of life, no substantial changes in the hearts and habits of our people will follow the most thoroughly organized program.

Nowhere in Scripture is there a condemnation of wealth, possessions, and earthly riches as such. Covetousness is not simply to have much. Our Lord Himself never excluded the rich from the kingdom of grace. He never shunned the man whose status and possessions were above the average. Possessions were not an automatic disqualification for saving faith, for Christ did not see sin and evil in things by themselves.

Possessions and wealth are a great blessing when used as God's will directs. The New Testament gives several examples where good and faithful stewardship of material possessions resulted in special commendation. If then it is not the possessions themselves which are evil, most certainly it is the *possessive attitude within man* about his goods which God condemns. Possessiveness does not lie in coins or dollars, or what they may purchase. It lies rather in the heart of the one who clings to things and wants more. This is Paul's emphasis: "The *love* of money is the root of all evil" (1 Tim. 6:10). The story of Ananias and Sapphira uncovers the sinful, possessive hearts of people. The rich ruler in Matthew 20 excluded himself from discipleship because his possessions ruled him.

Covetousness is not merely an infrequent sin which requires periodic confession to keep it under control. It becomes an actual way of living, disguised in man's natural aspiration "to get ahead." In the face of Luke 12:15 materialism declares its life-premise: "Life *does* consist in the abundance of the things which a man possesses!" And from this premise follows every other major life-drive: (1) *The purpose for living* is wrapped up in the needs of self; (2) *the incentive for living* is to accumulate "enough" stuff to assure personal satisfaction and security; (3) *the reward of life* is to enjoy the comfort and pleasure which one's storehouse provides.

Materialism is a universal disease. It does not depend on a political climate. It does not afflict only a particular race. Consequently its ever-present and ever-increasing image in America and around the world tends to give the appearance of an indestructible monster. Frequently it appears as if Christianity's counterthrust is destined to be nothing more than a hopeless attempt to compete.

Accordingly the church develops a type of "sanctified materialism" as man's religion; the emphasis is placed on beautiful, comfortable facilities for the faith: an abundance of social activities, athletic outlets for all ages, and a public relations creed calculated to make the church as attractive as the nearest country club or recreational facility. Christian giving in this setting is supposed to result because the church member is made aware that his church affords him just as much as any secular institution — with a little spiritual frosting besides.

Covetousness has its roots in the ground of not believing God. Facing this truth is a step in the direction of whittling the monster down to size. Tracing covetousness to the root of unbelief is far from contrived. When our Lord addressed Himself to this sin in the Sermon on the Mount, He graphically illustrated God's care for man. (He even cares for the lilies of the field and the sparrows of the sky.) Yet man continues to persist in worry and concern for himself. Without making an outright declaration, man frets for himself because he cannot fully believe that God knows how to order and

75

distribute the world's wealth to people. Worry is man's silent assertion that he must undertake this task for God.

Not only is the wisdom of God in His creation questioned by the coveting heart, but the loving preservation the Father promises His children is also suspect. The psalmist expresses his faith in the words: "O Lord, Thou preservest man and beast. How excellent is Thy loving kindness, O God! Therefore the children of men put their trust under the shadow of Thy wings." (36:6,7)

Beyond this the final act of unbelieving idolatry occurs. Once God as sovereign Creator and Preserver is discarded, the road is clear for self to ascend to the throne of life. Covetousness ultimately carries man this far — that he will assert the necessity and right to carve out his own life by a set of rules completely unrelated to his relationship to God through Jesus Christ.

In many instances Christians do not even recognize the seed of covetousness in their lives — much less acknowledge the flowering of a materialistic philosophy for their existence. For them giving remains a harsh duty and a heavy burden, and a most convincing presentation of the budget needs of the church will not really convince them. The problem for them is *not* that they fail to understand the cost of light and heat, sending missionaries, printing literature, and training workers. Their problem is still their unfamiliarity with the struggle between God and money in their own hearts.

The Gospel which calls and then moves Christians to follow God's plan also arms them well to wrest life out of the clutches of covetousness. It is this Gospel that will strike covetousness with full force and hammer loose its suffocating grip on Christian hearts and lives.[3]

Our Financial Investments and Offerings
for the Savior's Kingdom

Experience has shown that personal stewardship finds its acid test in the offerings people set aside for the work of the church. God has a definite plan for providing financial gifts for the work of His kingdom, but there is a great deal of ignorance of this plan on the part of His people. Some give from worldly considerations and motives, in disproportionate amounts, irregularly, infrequently, unwillingly, and not as unto God but as unto men. While these people may feel a vague guilt, they would suggest this is due to the pressure which the church exerts rather than to a need on their part to increase their giving. The stewardship committee chairman of a congregation writes: "Since becoming associated with the stewardship committee, I have been appalled by the evident lack of understanding demonstrated by too many members of our congregation. Some of us forget what we are really here for and the work we are to do." A pastor writes that the negative attitude and the lack of consecration of many members indicates a sick spiritual condition which, if not checked, could mean serious spiritual problems or even spiritual death for some of them. Church leaders will have to ask themselves how much of this problem comes from their failure to provide an effective message.

Many members live with a superficial understanding of Christian giving. Some people can see themselves as good stewards when they have "sacrificed" an hour's sleep on Sunday and have given one more dollar for the church program. They have learned to live with the criticism that such givers and such lives are not good or responsible stewardship. Somehow they have become immune to all types of criticism, and they never have been able to see the personal application of stewardship. Stewardship leaders can keep on repeating truisms while certain members keep their false conceptions. Such members generally will not awaken unless they are led to see the real motivation and plan for giving; they must learn that the church will go on without their offerings, for they now believe the church cannot survive without their money, even though the amount is small. This heresy exists in the minds of multitudes throughout Christendom, and it needs to be met with a broadside attack.

When a person does not give or serve happily, he is indicating by his actions that he has a spiritual problem. He usually covers it up by projecting his negative feelings on the congregation and its leaders while convincing himself that the real problem rests on the congregation, "which is too demanding." He gets the feeling that he is being visited so that the Every Member Stewardship Visit effort will be successful and that the congregation is not really interested in him as a person; thus much resentment is built up. Many people would acquire new images of their congregations and of the Kingdom if the stewardship messages summoned them to evangelical repentance and renewal instead of being a summons to buy a share in a church program.

T. K. Thompson tells about the need for deeper understanding when he writes: "Much of the giving of North American Protestants is based upon the sheer abundance and prosperity of the economy. This is not to say that there is no real sacrifice, or no depth of theological concern, or loyalty to Jesus Christ as divine Lord and Savior. It is to say that most North Americans can afford to be generous and out of the affluence of their situation they are glad to toss off 1 or 2 percent of their income. A deeper motivation and a deeper theological understanding of loyalty to Jesus Christ is necessary." [4] An effective message is required to perform this task.

The urge comes from concerned pastors and laymen alike to identify the basics of the message of Christian giving. A layman from Ohio writes: "My talks with individuals reveal a woeful lack of knowledge of God's plan and His promises. Sad to say we often do not get beyond almost trite statements about the love of Christ and the budget. Individuals must be led by the hand to understand what it means to put Christ first and to believe that God is able to provide all our needs over and above our gifts to Him." A pastor from New York writes: "The church is organized for the ingathering of money. But it often strikes me that there is really no vital connec-

78

tion at all between the giving and collecting on the one hand and the teaching and preaching and the believing on the other."

What can leaders say and do to avoid the impression that they are after church dollars just as others are after their marketing, housing, and insurance dollars, but rather show that they are after the man? What can we do for those who express their gratitude verbally but stop short of active obedience in daily living and Christian giving? What is the message of Christian giving for responsibility in personal stewardship? We now turn our attention to these questions.

A. *Basics and Principles in Christian Giving*

Christians need to learn the fundamentals of Christian giving. These are the considerations:

1. Know the meaning of money, which is received in exchange for use of time and abilities. Money is a trust from God. One hundred percent is to be spent to the glory of God for spiritual, physical, and other needs. These truths should be taught to all members. This very important matter is developed in an educational program that involves the use of two filmstrips ("That's Where the Money Goes!"), a book ("Where Does the Money Go?"), a budget plan, and a flip-chart ("Why Does God Give Men Money?"); the title of the whole package is "Where Does the Money Go?" [5]

2. Giving is an expression of love. "Prove the sincerity of your love." (2 Cor. 8:8)

3. Giving is a part of worship —Ps. 96:8. God's plan in Christ gives a sacred quality to the financial gift, for in love it becomes an offering of self. To dispose of church finances as mere collections is to tarnish an act that is a part of worship. The root of the offering is the saving relation of man to Christ, and the offering itself is an act of worship. Milo Kauffman asserts that Paul did not suddenly descend from the mountain heights of the resurrection in 1 Cor. 15 to the depths of the valley of a "collection" in chapter 16. Paul lost

no altitude in the transition from the resurrection to the offering. People should respond to the glorious truths of the Gospel in acts of worship. God pity the preacher who makes remarks like this: "After such an uplifting and inspiring message we hesitate having an offering." Such a statement detracts from the message. The thoughtful minister might say: "One could find no more fitting time to take an offering. We will now continue our worship as we offer our financial gifts." [6] Giving, as all of stewardship, has its origin in the love of God, and it is a response to that love.

4. Generous giving is a grace or gift from God — 2 Cor. 8:1, 2.

5. Basic problems in the matter of giving are a lack of knowledge, faith, and love; a false sense of values; and covetousness. God is concerned about attitudes. The church's needs are not the measure of our gifts. Avoid bad standards in giving. Not to give or to give little is a sin — Mal. 3:8; Luke 12:48. We are giving *from* blessings, not *to* a budget. We give *from* a loving heart, not *to* an empty budget.

6. Matt. 6:33 (Seek the Lord first) is the goal of all life, also Christian giving, and is a natural expression of faith. Give the firstfruits, not leftovers.

7. Give as God has given — 1 Cor. 16:2. Give weekly or regularly, give a generous percentage. Love and faith will set the percentage. You cannot give from what you don't have, only from what you *do* have — 2 Cor. 8:12.

8. Firstfruit, or generous percentage giving, is a plan for all of God's people. It is required in stewards that they be found faithful — 1 Cor. 4:2.

In his classic statements on Christian giving in 2 Cor. 8 and 9 St. Paul cites some basic principles for Christians to consider in their giving. V. S. Azariah summarizes the message of these chapters in the following manner: Giving is a grace and is intimately connected with the state of the spiritual life, an evidence of God's gracious work in the hearts of men (8:1). Affliction is no obstacle and poverty is no barrier to generous giving; it is always and everywhere true that giving does not depend upon wealth (8:2). The standard of giving must bear a recognized proportion to income, but this proportion must be fixed by the giver himself and not by others, for giving must be spontaneous and voluntary (8:3). Giving means fellowship in service, where the giver becomes a sharer in the work of God (8:4). Self-giving precedes the offering (8:5). Giving is a Christian grace, and the leaders must see to it that Christians increase in this grace also (8:7). Giving cannot be commanded by man's authority, but must be spontaneous and free; it can only be commended on spiritual grounds (8:8). Christian giving is based not on certain Old Testament passages or on the Mosaic legislation, but on the supreme self-giving of God Himself through our Lord Jesus Christ; the model and measure for Christian giving is Christ's giving (8:9). It is a function of the church's ministers to enable Christians for their own sake to fulfill their giving privileges and to do so with facility; a willing mind is the big requisite, and a Christian should give from what he has, not from what he does not have (8:10-12). Christian giving means Christian fellowship and sharing. Those who have been blessed will consider it their privilege to share with their fellow Christians who are in distress (8:13-14). A healthy example in giving is proper, for others thrill over evidences of love (8:24; 9:1-4). God does not urge Christian giving on grounds of reward, but generous giving brings rich rewards by grace (9:8-14). No giving of ours can be an adequate return for the wonderful gift of God. The Christian is urged to give because he has been redeemed by the precious blood of Christ and has received the gift of all gifts — God's grace in Christ Jesus in the forgiveness of sins (9:15).[7]

To help people consider seriously the expression of their faith through Christian giving we might pose the following questions: (1) Does all my spending show a Christian sense of value? (2) Do my offerings represent the firstfruits of my income? (3) Are spiritual causes given the priority? (4) Are my offerings made in love to Jesus, who is the Receiver of these gifts? (5) Are my offerings the full measure of my faith and love for Christ? (6) Are my offerings a generous portion or percentage of my income? (7) Am I willing to live without some of the luxuries of our American life in order to share a larger portion of my goods with the Master? (8) Am I willing now to increase my personal giving by 1 or 2 percent of my income if I am giving over 10 percent? (9) Am I willing now to increase my offerings by 3 or 4 percent or more if I am giving less than 10 percent?

The following illustration will help indicate the relevancy of proportionate giving. Mr. "X" earns $110 a week. He gives $2.50 a week for spiritual causes. This represents about 2 percent of his income. Mr. "Z" earns the same wages and gives 11 percent of his income while Mr. "X" gives 2 percent. What is the difference between the two men? Not the financial circumstances. The difference must be in spiritual understanding, love, and faith. Many Christians are giving more than 10 percent of their income to Christ and are being richly blessed. Some Christians are going far beyond with God's help and are still "making a living." If Mr. "X" by faith would give at least 10 percent, he would learn the spiritual law the remaining $99 would have more worth to him than the original $110. The nonspiritual mind cannot grasp this truth, but it is true, as many Christians have learned.

There is the problem of figuring the basis for planned percentage giving. Does one figure from the gross or net income? There will not be great difficulty in determining the basis for the percentage when the heart and mind are kept open for prayerful consideration of the question. The *attitude* is the starting place as one begins to figure the percentage. The method of operation must be left to individual judgment and to an enlightened conscience; we believe that Matt. 6:24-34 warrants the following principles.

Two extremes should be avoided. The first is to deduct all living expenses from one's income before determining the percentage for the Lord. God asks for the firstfruits, not for a percentage of what is left after His people have had their fill. The second extreme is the view that a farmer or businessman should give his percentage from his whole income before deducting legitimate costs of operating his business.

A straight salary and hourly pay present the simplest situation for figuring in the practice of firstfruit, i.e., proportionate giving. The wage earner or salaried person ordinarily carries none of the business expense and receives his pay regularly. There is no expense which might be legitimately regarded as a business expense for him, aside from transportation to and from work by one who has a problem of extreme distance. The salaried man and wage earner do not give from the take-home pay, but from the gross salary. The withholding law simply provides for the payment of one's income tax in advance. The proportionate giver will give from the income before such deductions are made.

The businessman or merchant will include as part of his business expenses such items as the purchase price of the stock on his shelves, clerk's salaries, heat and light for the store, insurance on the stock, business rent and taxes, and losses on uncollectible accounts. If he purchases or owns the building, he will not figure its cost or depreciation, because these become his assets and are not part of his current expenses. Thus he gives from an *adjusted* net income, subtracting only operating expenses.

The farmer should not find it any more difficult to arrive at his *adjusted* net income than the merchant or manufacturer. Expenditures for making the farm productive will be charged up to business expense. These items include rent, hired labor, repairs, seed, fertilizer, gas, and machine rental. He would not list as deductions such items as cost of the farm or extra acreage, new buildings, depreciation, and other such costs, for these items involve a person's assets and not his income. True, assets are needed in order to make money. However, offerings to God are not to wait until assets have been accumulated at the expense of His work. The farmer should also count as income foodstuffs received from the farm and used by the farmer himself, such as vegetables, meat, eggs, and milk.

Net income is not counted exactly as the income tax returns allow. Some of the deductions allowed by the government should be counted as personal living expenses in figuring the basis for proportionate giving. It doesn't pay to "drive a hard bargain" with the Lord. It is well to give God the benefit of the doubt on any questions concerning deductions before figuring the Lord's portion. This is the way of grace.

The farmer and the businessman will have some difficulty knowing what their current income is until they have figured their total income and expenses at the end of the year. They might follow the example of some farmers who are proportionate givers. These farmers average up their income of the past two or three years and then for the first 10 months give on the basis of this average. This would provide a good guideline for farmers (and businessmen), unless there are unusual circumstances. At the end of the year they would make up the difference after they have made a final accounting of their income.

It might even be well to figure the basis of one's percentage to the Lord, as someone has suggested, in this manner: If a person were promised a bonus of one tenth of his income, how would he figure his income? The only way to figure the income is to act the part of a child of God.

All spending and budgeting is very much a spiritual business and requires much flexibility. More than a formula of conduct, it is a way of life. To figure proportionate giving, all that is needed besides an understanding of the matter is: a pencil, a sheet of paper, and a willing heart — nothing more. There is an abundance of pencils and paper. God will provide the willing heart. Where there is a willing heart, there will not be disproportionate but proportionate giving.

B. *Priorities Are to Be Settled*

William J. Keech writes: "How many of our frustrations and defeats grow out of our unresolved loyalties! . . . When the problem of priority is settled, another one will be settled too; that is, the problem of unifying, or integrating life. Many feel that life holds for them an irritating complex of demands and challenges." [8]

In Matt. 6:33 Jesus exhorts man to seek the Lord first in the use of his time, abilities, and money, and to set for himself spiritual priorities and values. This is the New Testament principle of living. Unless God is at the center of man's life, an idol stands there in God's place, and to it all things and life itself are offered.

Efforts that teach giving should be designed to produce first the giving of the heart, of the self ("first they gave themselves," 2 Cor. 8:5). This point is sometimes stressed in order to produce more money for the church, but this should not be its first significance. The man who first gives himself to the Lord uses all his money for God, but this does not mean all for his congregation. In the degree that he spends for the physical necessities of his family and for all spiritual and charitable causes *as a Christian man,* he indicates he has first given himself.

In a time of shifting values God's people need to learn that good desires can be met without an indulgent yielding to fleshly appetites and that life is unbalanced unless God comes first. There should be a proper emphasis on the spiritual and internal aspects of the Christian life, not overemphasizing the material at the cost of the spiritual factors. We are engaged in a restive search for meaning in modern life, and we must find significance and purpose for our activities and work. In the midst of it we should be asked, "What are your goals in life?" and then we should hear Christ's own challenge of Matt. 6:33: "Seek ye first the kingdom of God and His righteousness, and all these things [food, drink, clothes] will be added unto you." [9]

C. Investing Money for Greater Outreach

If our personal stewardship is truly understood and man's relationship to material blessings perceived, then stewardship of money will go even beyond spending it wisely on self and giving generously to the work of the Kingdom. What about savings? Is it proper to build up estates and amass fortunes in secular investments while needed investments for God's "building and loan" program are lacking?

Much of the work of home missions these days gets its real foundation from loans for building adequate facilities. The loan agency of some church bodies is called Church Extension or God's Bank. This is the church's "building and loan association," which offers loans to mission groups that are incapable of getting a loan from a commercial agency because of the lack of collateral. But where does God's Bank or the Church Extension Fund get the money to make the loans? Obviously it comes from people who invest in the church's building program. God's Bank offers not only financial interest but also spiritual rewards. When we talk about stewardship we are also talking about savings and investments.

When churches are to be built and congregations must go to God's Bank, are Christian savings always available? Are savings working for the Lord and ready to be lent for such great purposes, or are they all invested in commercial ventures that may reap greater financial gains? Savings in God's Bank are an act of wise stewardship. A Christian will not invest all his savings in commercial ventures while the Church Extension Fund is unable to grant adequate loans to congregations in need of new buildings.

And what about estates and wills? Are estates to be left

only to children in order that they may use them also for secular purposes? Or should provision be made to leave a substantial part of the estate to the work of the Kingdom? When we talk about stewardship, we are also talking about making a will: a *Christian* will.

The use of savings for church building and the writing of Christian wills is a dimension of Christian stewardship that has been neglected by many members. Church bodies have engaged in active promotional efforts in both areas, but the message has not been put into practice among most members. There are some stewardship leaders in congregations who discourage a program of education in both areas because they are more concerned with the annual budget and somehow feel that the "savings program" might take away money from the current program. There is much evidence of a lack of clarity in the relationship of stewardship to these two areas.

Savings in God's Bank and making a Christian will — these are also personal stewardship! They fit well into God's Gospel plan. They are all tied up in one neat package. They call for coverage in regular stewardship efforts. Indeed they should not be separated from stewardship messages and programs.

D. Is Tithing Part of Our Personal Stewardship?

There is little question that some tithing programs of the past have been distinct blessings to certain people in a way that awakened them to a joyful partnership with God. However it appears that often this spiritual growth came as a result of an organized effort where God's grace worked through the overall education program apart from the tithing challenge itself. The tithing emphasis filled in the void where an effective educational program in proportionate giving was long overdue. Today tithing needs to be reevaluated on the basis of Biblical theology.

The Old Testament believers brought 10 percent plus

thankofferings to God, and they were blessed. Under the grace of the New Testament and out of love for Christ what shall we give as our offerings to God? Many early Christians gave more than 10 percent, although God did not demand it. Some feel that the tithe is the answer to financial problems. "The tithe is the Lord's," they say. When God commanded the tithe in the Old Testament, this was regarded as an expression of loving worship and demonstrated a sincere concern to fulfil God's plan for the proper conduct of worship and for the proper care of widows, orphans, and the needy. Should the Christian demonstrate his love in a different way in his giving? The Old Testament shows various examples that the believers should tithe, but the New Testament does not require exactly one tenth for the Lord's work! *Christian* stewardship recognizes not only a tenth but all as belonging to God, and man acts as the trustee of all. New Testament giving is not a hard and cold fact set down by a law of arithmetic and rigid decimals, but it is the practice of love.

T. A. Kantonen provides these Scriptural insights on tithing: "The greatest danger has been to compromise the Gospel through moralism and legalism drawn from the Old Testament. Thus the tithe has assumed a far greater prominence than it has in the New Testament and has often been advocated on grounds quite different from the spirit of the Gospel. . . . If the aim of stewardship were only to achieve practical results, such as the securing of money for a worthy cause, any kind of theology serving this purpose would be justified. . . . When people ask how much they should give, the theology of the Gospel does not permit us to reply simply, 'The Word of God has the answer. You must give a tenth of your income. You must tithe, for God has commanded it.' . . . The Lord gave no command concerning the tithe. . . . We see the superficiality of the view that tithing is the one divinely authorized and unconditionally binding method for practicing Christian stewardship. Not only does it lack a New Testament foundation but it lends

88

itself to a man-centered legalism which imperils true religion."[10]

Some of the arguments for tithing sound quite convincing, and the whole matter can be spelled out very logically. However, the challenge of the tithe itself (the exact 10 percent, for it has no other meaning) falls flat when the Christian asks, "*Who* says I must give exactly 10 percent?" Christ is no new lawgiver, and He does not command 10 percent of any one person any more than an exact 9 or 11 percent. Love does not have a mathematical standard, nor does it fix certain rates or limits. And what becomes of Christian growth and sanctification when we peg everyone's faith at 10 percent? Some may only have a 4 percent faith, if it could be known, and it would be very harmful to load their conscience with the force of a law that says that they must now give 10 percent.

We should keep in mind what Jesus had to say about the tithe, always in the context of speaking to Pharisees. St. Paul, insisting that Christians were not under law but under grace, sought "to get away from an external code and to move in the inner realm of man's response to the grace of God in Christ," writes Holmes Ralston. "There is a grave danger that in the preaching of the tithe we shall fall into a type of legalism which is not essentially different from the Jewish legalism which Paul rebelled against." [11]

Perhaps one of the major emphases in the Pharisee's life was to show his dedication to God and His Law by tithing, and even double-tithing at times. Paul could describe himself as a Pharisee of the Pharisees, trained at the feet of Gamaliel. Although some of those whom the apostle addressed were Jewish Christians, he nowhere says anything about tithing. He has a lot to say about giving as God has given and giving oneself completely to God in view of that tremendous divine love, but nowhere does he betray his Pharisaic training in an emphasis on the exact 10 percent or tithe.

Helge Brattgård asserts: "According to Professor T. A.

Kantonen, the interpretation of Malachi 3:10 has played a calamitous role in a number of American churches. In this way the old heathen worship formula: *do ut des*, has smuggled itself in, in spite of what church leaders have done to prevent it. The New Testament texts do not recognize any binding law as an answer to the question of how much the Christian should give." [12]

Tithing is a commendable practice, but it must be handled carefully since it has no specific New Testament sanction. Undoubtedly tithing is a virtue, but it should be sought by a person *on his own initiative*. It cannot be *urged on others* as the will of God for them. It is not a virtue like honesty; it is a degree of a virtue, and leaders should not press degrees of virtues on people. Believers *grow* in such virtues.

The tithe is not man's real problem. His real problem lies in putting God first and giving generously. God's grace will take over *after* that, too, and give the faith to go beyond 10 percent. Most people have real spiritual problems and attitudes to change and conquer first before they can think about tithing.

God gives each of His children the responsibility of determining the separated portion in the light of conscience, faith, and the promptings of love, instead of arbitrarily fixing a uniform proportion for all under all circumstances. Under most circumstances true love for Christ might constrain the Christian to adopt a standard of giving *higher* than that of the Hebrew law. Under all circumstances the tenth part is but an example only.

Out of gratitude for the free gift of salvation, shall not the Christian desire to bring freely a higher percentage of his income than the Old Testament believer under the Law? Was not everything that Jesus touched enlarged and spiritualized? The fact that there is no definite New Testament law for the Christian to give a tithe does not lessen his responsibility to act, because he is under grace and on his honor. While the example of the faithful both in the Old and the New Testament may be a guide, we look only at what Jesus did for men and then ask, "In the light of such sacrifice for me, what percentage will I give?" Will it be 7, 10, 11, 13 percent? More? Less? Love and faith will set the percentage.

Freedom to Arrange Life in Response to the Call

Personal stewardship raises delicate issues about our Christian liberty and our relationship to the group. We are not called to be stewardship manikins that perform specific tasks and adopt certain habits at the impulse of others. Even though there is a great need for interaction between members of the body, this fellowship is of free persons bound together by a common calling for mutual edification. This edification is based on God's call, not on other's estimates of what should be done. There are great needs for abilities and money in the church. What is the balance of responsibility between the individual and the group? What freedom does the individual have to order his own stewardship life?

We are free only as we are bound to God, only as we keep looking to Him. Before the new birth we are free only to choose which false gods we will serve and what priority we will give to earthly scales of values. Through our regeneration we share creatively in the unfolding plan of God.

Union with Christ brings us into a freedom unknown by the natural man, as Paul shows when he writes of "the liberty wherewith Christ hath made us free" (Gal. 5:1). "Being then made free from sin, ye became the servants of righteousness" (Rom. 6:18). Luther told of the paradox of being free and slave at the same time when he said that the Christian is the most free lord of all and subject to none, even while he is the most dutiful servant of all and subject to everyone. Freedom releases the believer for greater service than he could possibly render under regimentation. Christian liberty makes Christian service complete in a way no law or rule could ever do it. Liberty under grace gives personal stewardship a quality by the indwelling Christ utterly beyond that which could be forced by the best-regulated conditions set down in the Law itself.

When the balance of the individual's pricelessness and of corporate responsibility is tampered with, the unity of man in Christian freedom is violated. The temptation is always present to emphasize either the individuality or the corporateness at the expense of or complete exclusion of the other. Man will endure the indignities of pressure and legalistic measures for a time, but either his conscience will become deadened to personal responsibility or he will be headed for an explosion.

We can never accept the idea that the Christian is incompetent and irresponsible to the degree that he needs to be told what his decisions must be. No genuine communication can be established if love is held in the straitjacket of regulations and if human values are forgotten. Human values are disregarded when man is regarded as a means for achieving organizational goals and then is organized for such achievement. Human relations deteriorate when one individual tries to lord it over others in urging conclusions on them before they have had a chance to think through all the alternatives. In fact there must be the freedom to fail, to make mistakes, and to learn lessons by a few mistakes; the alternative is a false security which believes that manipulation is assurance of success. Suzanne de Dietrich says: "Only in Christ can we solve the tension between freedom and authority, between the right of the individual person to attain fulness of life and the claim of the community as a whole on each of its members." [13]

Rachel Henderlite tells how life in the New Covenant is a life of freedom. She writes: "One who is forgiven is set free of condemnation and guilt, set free to live in covenant with God and man. . . . He is free from guilt so that he can look another in the face without shrinking back, free from shame so that he can move out toward every man with head erect, free from covetousness so that he can give to another without thereby giving up the structure of his life in the root of security, free from the necessity to resist and attack and dominate. The acceptance of forgiveness sets a man *free to* as well as *free from.* It sets him free to absorb hostility instead of resisting it, free to forgive evil instead of returning it, free to trust another instead of suspecting, free to serve instead of being served. This is the mark of the man who lives under the ethics of justification by faith. . . . His freedom does not mean liberty to do what he pleases. It means freedom to do what God pleases. Freedom in Christ is not undirected liberty. It is covenant with God in Christ, bondage to God." [14]

Enslavement to self results when we refuse to serve God. Serving self or the demands of other people in small matters day by day is slavery on the installment plan. Christ purchased our freedom from that sort of life. The Gospel that makes us free also makes us responsible. There is the freedom of the Gospel, but there are also restraints of the Gospel.

There is always the danger that we will abuse, misuse, or despise our freedom and the Gospel message. Personal stewardship suggests the rhythmic pulsations of worship and witness, of learning and response. Our lives should be flexible, with many variations and shifts to match our uniqueness and individuality as God intended us to be. Though we may have the same degree of faith and commitment, each of us will react differently in the same situation. One may show "holy impatience" while another expresses "holy patience," each acting according to his own characteristics and potentiality.

Some situations present difficult choices, especially when urgent demands are made upon the church to perform. We owe something to God, His church, and ourselves; these should never be placed in competition with one another.

93

When we feel the demand for immediate success, we tend to make demands on others to conform to the will of the group. Helmut Thielicke reminds us that necessity is not pitted against freedom.[15] Christian dignity is destroyed to the degree that we measure a member by his achievement as a producer. Thielicke states: "The functionary is not himself when he acts. He is simply an organ carrying out orders. Something else or someone else is exercising his will 'through him.'"[16] We must recall that our authority to function in a congregation is a delegated authority and that in our authority we are answerable to God.

To misconstrue Christian liberty means to exchange that liberty for a form of slavery and to crush people as rights are wrongfully claimed. Thielicke writes: "Dreams that are constantly checked, examined, and bombarded with regimentation, and thus cannot flow freely, are not dreams at all, but only anxious spasms."[17]

Notes for Chapter 5

[1] Dietrich Bonhoeffer, *The Cost of Discipleship* (New York: Macmillan, 1960), p. 82.

[2] Helge Brattgard, *God's Stewards*, trans. Gene Lund (Minneapolis: Augsburg, 1963), p. 68.

[3] Some of this section was taken from a presentation by the Rev. Calvin Fiege, Ann Arbor, Mich., at stewardship schools which the author directed in Detroit and Grand Rapids, Mich., in July 1963.

[4] T. K. Thompson, *Christian Stewardship and Ecumenical Confrontation* (National Council of the Churches of Christ, Department of Stewardship and Benevolence, 1961), p. 40.

[5] St. Louis: Church-Craft Pictures, 1964.

[6] Milo Kauffman, *The Challenge of Christian Stewardship* (Scottdale, Penn.: Herald Press, 1955), p. 12.

[7] V. S. Azariah, *Christian Giving* (New York: Association Press, 1955), pp. 64-75.

[8] William J. Keech, *The Life I Owe* (Valley Forge: Judson Press, 1948), p. 15.

[9] Priorities and firstfruits are discussed at length in Chap. 8, *Where Does the Money Go?* See note 5.

[10] T. A. Kantonen, *A Theology for Christian Stewardship* (Philadelphia: Muhlenberg Press, 1956), pp. 6, 9, 21, 23.

[11] Holmes Ralston, *Stewardship in the New Testament* (Richmond: John Knox Press, 1946), p. 23.

[12] Brattgard, p. 92.

[13] Suzanne de Dietrich, *The Witnessing Community* (Philadelphia: Westminster Press, 1958), pp. 13, 14.

[14] Rachel Henderlite, *Forgiveness and Hope* (Richmond: John Knox Press, 1961), p. 79.

[15] Helmut Thielicke, *The Freedom of the Christian Man* (New York: Harper & Row, 1962), p. 17.

[16] Thielicke, p. 156.

[17] Thielicke, p. 63.

Chapter 6

The Ministry of Group Stewardship

We have a ministry to one another to help us develop our stewardship response to the covenant call of God. This ministry helps the congregation live out the calling of the covenant. The objective of this ministry is to attain a growing number of people who worship and serve Christ, our Savior. "Go and teach" is one of the chief functions of the church's ministry to fulfill this objective. As people are taught, they are brought to faith, strengthened in that faith, and express that faith.

H. G. Coiner writes: "That God has elected His people to be His agents of reconciliation is a claim made not *by* the church but *on* the church by its Lord. This claim is to be accepted humbly and fearfully by the Christian church. . . . The *nature* of the church as the reconciled community is inseparable from the *function* of the church as the agent, or minister, of reconciliation.[1]

Churches may have many committees, programs, organizations, and "campaigns" with members relentlessly pursuing a host of outward activities and stated objectives. Yet it is possible that their permanent impact on people is negligible. The first and great function is not to be active in the church "in some way," but rather to teach and edify one another in love through the Gospel of forgiveness. When someone asks, "Lord, what wilt Thou have me to do?" church leaders should take care not to intervene with easy answers that suggest functions which are less than what the Christian calling conveys.

What is the duty and the call for the group? The group, like the individual person, is called to Christian vocation under the covenant. Group goals, motivations, methods, and programs are always considered under this one principle.

The Group's Challenge to the Individual to Bear Fruit

The church as people is called to provide ministry to one another in expressing their Christian calling as servants of God. There can be no individualism that allows any member to go his own way and ignore his responsibility to the group or to deny the group's responsibility to him. "Edify one another" (1 Thess. 5:11). "Exhort one another daily" (Heb. 3:13). True stewardship can hardly be exercised, if there is little or no edification and ministry to one other by individual Christians.

The unity of believers in Christ involves such a close sharing of life that no one can be allowed to create his own personal universe apart from membership in the body. Other people's weaknesses and strengths are every Christian's business, and the individual's problems and blessings are the concern of other Christians. Evangelical discipline should help members make responsible decisions. This agrees with Paul's admonition: "Let no man seek his own good, but the good of his neighbor" (1 Cor. 10:24 RSV). 1 Corinthians 12 and Romans 12 tell of the mutual dependence of members.

Congregational leaders will be dismayed if any members slam doors in the face of visitors and deny a hearing to a message that seeks to edify them and further instruct them in God's great plan for them. If stewardship leaders have planned to minister to members according to the instructions of the Head of the church, then they have a right to be heard. All Christians need the stimulation of a living church fellowship if they are to grow toward maturity and faithfulness.

The Book of James allows no doubt as to the necessity of good works and fruits of faith on the part of all members. In Psalm 1 man is likened to a tree that bears fruit. John

15 shows Christians as branches attached to the Vine, and they bear the fruit that the Vine produces. Faith without works is dead but from a living faith church leaders may expect growth, development, and spiritual progress.

We cannot allow weak and lame excuses for not producing good works or for continuing in unrestrained, sinful ways. Some may feel: "My case is different; my human, physical, and material resources are so little that I must be excused." Much room must be left for individuality and variations in faith and action. Yet God's promise is to all believers, and fruit in one degree or another is to be expected in the lives of the weak and the strong, the learned and the unlearned. Even though there are practical considerations to be heeded, we must avoid the temptation to treat people as *segments of a classified group* in the congregation (lower one third, middle one third, upper one third, etc.) instead of *spiritual beings* which have basic educational needs for direction in the church. Each member is a distinct individual with his own uniqueness for bearing the fruits of faith through the Gospel.

Byfield and Shaw point out the inconsistency of allowing any members to neglect their stewardship: "There is no room in Christianity for people who are unwilling to give of themselves. And this statement is made in love and for the sake of the people themselves. . . . Perhaps this points to a basic problem within so many of our churches: the fear that we may offend someone who is a member. How many sermons have been dulled just at the cutting edge . . . how many 'punches have been pulled' by stewardship committees for fear that 'someone might become angry' and leave the church! When one reads the New Testament . . . and realizes the standards that the great apostle held up for church membership, one wonders how the church has managed to develop this particular fear. . . . We often seem to assume that church membership is a sort of birthright. . . . If a person remains within the fellowship and at the same time eludes all of his

Christian responsibilities, he cannot help observing that this sort of behavior appears to be condoned. Particularly is this true if, when he appears to be offended at something that has been said, the minister and parishioners hasten to apologize to him and to soothe his tender feelings. Is it any wonder after treatment like this that he gradually subsides into a nominal sort of relationship in which nothing bothers him because nothing touches him and in which, by the expedient of sitting in his pew, he is rendered immune to the Gospel in any way in which it might touch his life." [2]

Jesus wants fruit, not excuses for not bearing fruit. God's attitude toward a useless Christian life is manifested by His curse of the barren fig tree (Luke 13:6,7). The fig tree, planted in the vineyard for bearing fruit, failed utterly in the purpose for which it was planted. Evidently some Christians are failing in their function in the blessed vineyard of the church. They do not commit open and vicious sins. Socially and morally their lives may be unimpeachable. The great tragedy with them is that their lives are barren of the real fruits of the Christian life. God will just as surely curse a life for its fruitlessness as bless a life for its fruitfulness. Because He made them for service, it is improper to give the impression that God will accept their baskets of excuses for not serving Him.

Christ shows He is concerned about the reaction to His call to group stewardship. He said: "Now, what do you think of this? A man had two sons. He went to the first and said, 'Son, go and work in the vineyard today.' 'I won't,' he answered. Later he changed his mind and went. The father went to the other one and told him the same thing. He answered, 'I will, sir,' but didn't go. Which of the two did what the father wanted? They answered, 'The first.' Jesus said to them, 'I tell you the truth, tax collectors and prostitutes are going into God's kingdom ahead of you." (Matt. 21:28-31, Beck)

None should be allowed to escape an acute sense of

stewardship — to remain an immature, helpless, and whimpering baby who feels that he is doing God a favor by going to church, communing, and giving small offerings. Where there is no self-discipline, the fellow Christians are expected to discipline that person. Love for a person suggests that his weaknesses be brought to his attention. A fig tree must be pruned periodically if it is to bear fruit. If the tree were human, it would probably cry out in pain over this operation. But the fact that the unfruitful branches are pruned saves the tree and makes it more fruitful. This pruning is less "painful" than to carry heavy dying branches which would eventually result not only in unfruitfulness but in the death of the tree itself. Personal stewardship demands helpfulness in the church toward the type of discipline that God desires in all Christians.[3]

The Goals of the Group Ministry

Congregations are constantly under call to examine their work and to set their sights for their group stewardship. Their concern for each individual causes them to agree on goals which they hope to achieve in their educational ministry.

The chief educational goal of group stewardship is to present the Gospel message of God's grace in such a way that people who receive it can make proper decisions about it. The activities of stewardship must flow from the goals of Christian education. Through the Word of judgment and grace the goal is to help people see the connection between their life and its purpose, between spiritual values and their occupation, between their own needs and the needs of other people.

People are to be encouraged to seek righteousness and know how God defines that righteousness. They are to learn what it means to love God and their neighbor. Leaders are called to speak prophetically from the Word about the problems of materialism, about the insane chase after money and things, and about living in a stupor that puts a high price on possessions while forgetting moral and spiritual values. This does not mean lambasting national sins, but exposing personal faults and failures. This suffering world calls for a prophetic ministry and for a church of compassion.

The educational program should always reveal all of God's propositions of His plan for men. Programs tend to become localized in a feverish round of excitement over lesser concerns, such as gathering money for depleted treasuries. K. Kuntz advises: "When such a thorough program is developed, the money will come, but this is the result of a vital program and the securing of money must never dim the integrity of teaching and promotion of Christian stewardship." [4]

It must be decided what a valid goal is. Has the church any right to make its own institutional goals of primary importance or to substitute them for Biblical goals? Which is the proper goal: To win 25 unchurched people next year or to enlist and train all members as witnesses for the Lord Jesus through their daily lives and through the formal evangelism efforts of the church? To increase the budget by $14,000 next year, or to teach and challenge every Christian to bring the firstfruits and a proportionate share of his income to the Lord? We do not wish to say that it is wrong to desire 25 more new members next year and $14,000 more for the budget; we are saying that the goal that has real validity and Biblical sanction is the one that grows out of the Word, not out of man's hopes and desires for specific achievement and statistical increase.

A goal for a $14,000 increase next year may appeal more to emotional response than a goal of "every member a proportionate giver," but the dollar increase can be obtained without the change of giving habits or attitudes on the part of a single church member. Our goal is changed people, not bigger budgets.

The valid goal is that goal which is (1) rooted in the

Word, (2) grows in the Word, and (3) grows out of the Word. The valid goal starts out in the Word, feeds on the Word, and will not go any farther than the Word has stated. This is not a static thing at all, but it is a growing, living, dynamic process, since the life-giving element of the Word is present in terms of the goal. The goal itself may grow, may expand and become larger, and may have more implications to it, but all of these are rooted in the Word. As the goal expands out from the Word into the life of which we are a part, it will never lose the relationship which it has to the Word.

Since goals for stewardship efforts are of utmost importance, "any goal that stops anywhere short of the fulness of Christ is shortsighted and stultifying, and the inadequacy of the goal will inevitably affect adversely the means, method, and motivation." [5] We believe that Biblical theology suggests that the following be considered as the specific goals of group stewardship (this includes general stewardship efforts and the EMSV):

1. Review briefly the Christian's true nature in Christ and show him his heritage as a child of God and a beneficiary of God's creative and regenerative power, the object of His divine love, the recipient of His infinite mercy, and the possessor of His promise of salvation and eternal life. Help the member to see his self-centered and covetous nature, but then point him to his new nature in Christ.

2. Show each Christian the obstacles that can prevent the spiritual growth God intends for him. Be sure he has an awareness of his fellowship in Christ and the reality of his Kingdom involvement in contrast to the drives and pulls of his human and earthly involvements.

3. Help each member to discover new spiritual insights and awaken a better understanding of Christian discipleship. Show him how the Word and sacraments are the source of power for Christian living, for witnessing in every situation, and for widened spiritual horizons.

4. Indicate how God has given him abilities to use faithfully in the Kingdom. Reveal what God says about the giving of time and money and that their use is an expression of faith and love.

5. Help him to understand his income and money as a trust from God, not a personal possession for which he has no accountability. Let him see that the possession of money does not involve rights as much as it involves a responsibility to God for wise use. Indicate how a Christian should manage the income and possessions which God has loaned him and discuss responsible spending and budgeting of his total income.

6. Cultivate the grace of firstfruit, generous, proportionate giving. Be assured that he knows what it means to give the firstfruits, to give a generous percentage of income to Christ, and to give in worship. Point out some of the misunderstandings and false conceptions about Christian giving. Reveal that a Christian gives not *to* a church budget or *to* man-calculated needs, but *from* the blessings which God has shared with him.

7. Show how Christian service and giving is a matter of having a joyful spirit and a faithful attitude which trusts God and commits one to the tasks of the Kingdom.

8. Encourage a commitment by all of the use of abilities in definite service and the adoption of responsible giving habits. Invite every Christian in the name of Jesus to "seek first the kingdom of God and His righteousness, and all these things [earthly needs] shall be added unto him" (Matt. 6:33). Invite decisions based on spiritual priorities in the use of abilities and income in daily life and in the church.

It should be noted that it is neither possible nor wise to include all eight points and the total stewardship concerns in every EMSV or in one educational program. The entire round of theology outlined in this book cannot be included in one stewardship effort. All the theological considerations should be implicit in every effort, however.

Coordinating Stewardship with the Total Parish Program

At what point does stewardship overlap education, evangelism, general soul care, and other primary spiritual concerns? Leaders of congregations need to define the specific responsibilities of each committee and each parish concern. Leaders must determine in their program where "stewardship" stops lest it become synonymous with all of systematic theology and the Christian life. We cannot let "stewardship" mean just "money," and we dare not make it cover everything involved in the Christian call or sanctification. Stewardship must be presented from a broad theological base, and it is precisely for this reason that it must be carefully coordinated and integrated with other responsibilities in the parish life.

Like the human body, the church is made up of many members with various functions. No member works independently; there is an intimate relationship between the members. The entire body functions as a unit, and each member contributes to the welfare of the others. The total educational program should be integrated so that there is cross-fertilization through all the emphases carried on within the congregation.

We have indicated the wide range of responsibilities which should be undertaken. This is not to say that the stewardship committee is to assume any greater part than other committees. Nor is it saying that all this is to be put into the stewardship *program*. All these matters are a part of the parish emphasis and as such should be noted by the elders or deacons, by the Christian education committee, and by other leaders. The stewardship committee should channel its deepest concerns through all the committees and organizations into the congregation.

The congregation's educational program should first train every member for family devotions, worship, Bible study, and witnessing. If visits to the homes and group meetings at church are used as means in the educational process, then the visits ought to include these matters too. As a ship's voyage is not complete until the cargo is delivered, so a congregational program is not successful until it is properly unified and then transmitted to the individual members.

The doctrine of the Christian call must shine through everything that is done in worship, education, pastoral care, counseling, evengelism, and stewardship. There is an absolute unity to the problem and the solution of the church's mission. It is not a simple matter. On the one hand people who do not have family devotions nor go to Bible class usually do not use the Word because they feel no need for the strength of the Word. Neither do they feel any need for home devotions and Bible class because they are not expressing their faith in a vital way which would demand going to God for such strength. They do not express their faith more actively because of a lack of understanding and a feeling of inability to perform.

In delinquent cases it is not just a matter of counseling to go to church. Church attendance has sometimes been pictured as the main good work, way out of proportion to Biblical theology. For example, divorce problems cannot be settled merely by telling the couple to go to church and to love each other more. At the level of faith in any problem case, faith may be expressed in stumbling steps of evangelism and stewardship expression. People need to be shown that the Word has the power to unite them in love and that the Word will also give them mutual interest in bringing the message of peace and pardon to others in the community and the world. People must be given such a purposeful picture of the Word that it not only helps to settle their own personal problems but also is a part of their ministry of reconciliation at the same time.

Perfect coordination in the complex work of the church is hardly possible, but effective coordination is to be sought. There is no reason for the stewardship group to work at cross purposes with other boards and committees, nor for others to work at variance with the stewardship committee. There is a wonderful harmony that binds all together in the work of the body. Leaders of different boards and committees should work together in approaches and educational emphases so that God's people may "grow up into Him in all things, which is the Head, even Christ." (Eph. 4:15)

The Ministry of the Stewardship Leader to the Group[6]

The stewardship leader begins his work where the people are and tries to lead them in the name of God to where God wants them to be. *Christ* is the Leader, and as He treated people, so the stewardship leader treats them. The leader accepts all members — strong and weak alike — for what they are, but he does not let them stay there.

The stewardship leader emphasizes the integrity of the individual and the fraternal demands of the fellowship. Stewardship performance is personal; it is the individual's trust; it is his decision, and he can never be allowed the costly flight to the crowd! The leader must direct the individual to seek comfort in the mercy of God, not in the company of fellow sinners where he will revert to the performance level of the group.

In the stewardship educational phase the leader begins with the individual and ends with the group. He starts with the "I" and ends with the "we" of stewardship. The "I" and "we" must be balanced — the "I" must be allowed to express himself while the "we" is carefully considered. The stewardship leader should recognize what is implied when the members consider their leaders the "they" group — an indication that leaders may not be communicating properly.

The stewardship leader does not try to scold God's people into godliness; instead he conveys a blessing for true piety. He has the *care* of the church, and he *confers* the blessing of God. He builds his bridges of understanding on the bedrock of God's plan for his people, and he assumes that the church is the church. The stewardship leader will recognize the subtle form of Pharisaism which believes that the leader is just a little more consecrated than others. The leader must believe that the individual believes.

The stewardship leader is distinguished by his restless patience and realistic optimism. He is thankful for what has been done by God's grace and hopeful for what will happen. The spirit of the Gospel is not pessimism. Man walks, but the Holy Spirit flies. The stewardship leader knows that the results are God's, not his. As he goes about his stewardship work, he asks himself, "Whose activity is this, and what results do we hope to achieve?"

The stewardship leader seeks to create and maintain an impression that will encourage expression. He should understand the long step from motivation to action. He must know the steps from the "why" to the "who" to the "what" to the "how." The "what" and the "how" must be settled but only on the basis of the "why" and the "who." [7]

Two Different Scenes in Group Stewardship

The unclear manner in which most members see their part in God's plan seems to indicate that congregations need better communication and messages. That the problem persists indicates the need for more serious searching and analyzing.

What is being communicated to God's priests? What is coming through to them as they sit in the pews, attend meetings, and receive EMSV callers? To what extent are Biblical concepts of Christianity, the church, the Christian vocation, and stewardship being understood?

Is the member being shown *God's* program or *ours?* Are we teaching him God's Word or asking him to serve and give on the basis of what we assume to be God's will based on the obvious needs of the church? The Christian call will be violated if we deal improperly with the individual especially in the matter of Christian service and giving. What a difference in these following two scenes:

Scene 1. Leaders beg a member to teach Sunday school or vacation Bible school or to serve as an officer or on a committee of some organization, and they plead with him to "sacrifice" a little bit of time to do his "share." He is told it will not take too much time and that the church needs the help very badly.

Scene 2. Leaders indicate that after prayerful consideration they have come to the conclusion that God has given this particular Christian some very specific talents to be used in one or another function in His kingdom. Leaders help the Christian to discover his abilities. They challenge him in the name of Christ to exercise the talents God has given him for the spiritual welfare of people God wants to reach through him. The individual is not pushed into accepting the leaders' proposition but is merely shown that leaders feel God has given abilities and that there are challenging opportunities to which his love may respond.

In one scene the church and Christ become beggars, while the other scene finds the church representing Christ in a teaching situation where people are reminded to function as God's priests according to God's gifts to them. Here are the two scenes once more as they pertain to giving:

Scene 1. Leaders come to a member to tell him about the work of his congregation and his wonderful church body. The budget or work program of the local group is recounted and told in glowing terms. Then he hears of the financial aspects of world missions, and he is urged to give a generous gift as a loyal member. He is told finally that these plans will be made possible if he will consider larger offerings or proportionate giving.

Scene 2. Leaders come as God's priests humbly to present a Scriptural message to another of His priests. He is told of God's great plan for him and what God has done to make this possible. He is helped to understand his dual nature: the factors and forces at work in him that make him covetous and that make him generous and how God has helped him through Christ to settle this problem. Rather than approaching him as one who is to supply the needs of his church, he is approached as a person whose union in Christ and faith is to be expressed in the use of all his possessions. Because giving habits are involved, the leaders have come to talk, not about what his church is doing, but about *him* and his need to consider the Scriptural truths of giving. He is told of the mercies of God and the truths about firstfruit, generous, percentage giving. He is shown that he is God's steward, a CHRIST-ian, not just a supporter of church programs. Through the Word he is encouraged towards attitudes, conduct, and commitment that effectively express his Christian faith. He is challenged to grow in the grace of proportionate giving and toward ever-deepening discipleship.

The first scene finds faith applied to church plans, while the second scene challenges faith to respond to the true terms of Christian discipleship. In one scene people will tend to get the impression that leaders are imposing their will and their ideas on them. In the other scene people see God speaking to them through their leaders. In the first scene the church places its attention on the external act; in the second scene the attention is on the internal condition. In one approach people are treated as supporters, while in the other as priests of God. In one approach current information is presented to motivate people for enlarged gifts, while in the other the Word is used as the means to build up their sanctification and teach the grace of giving. In the first way the church is a beggar, while in the other a proclaimer. One approach is the "we-they" concept, while the other makes it an "I-we" concept.

Reversal of Field

We propose that there be a complete reversal of field in the stewardship focus of the group ministry. The *complete reversal of approach* to members is this: instead of asking them to commit themselves to what the church feels it needs in terms of abilities and money, the church comes to the people to help them take inventory of their own abilities and encourages them to have these developed, enlisted, and used. When the church states its needs and tries to find the workers, it becomes a beggar and the worker becomes a supporter. When the church goes to the individual, it reminds him of his true worth and ministry to others and to the world according to the resources God has given him. *This is the only creative approach that will bring the diversity of talents into a true unity in the functioning body.*

This reversal of field will help the members to be true disciples and to function according to the gifts that God has given and that need to be discovered rather than having the church structure a skeleton organization that can be run only by begging for a few enthusiasts who respond to the call of church leaders. *In this approach there will be an open-ended form that is as fluid as God's word is dynamic!* In congregational meetings this approach will find leaders discussing how they can help all Christians to discover their abilities and use them faithfully rather than spinning their wheels in heated talks about how they can get more people active in jobs that have been begging for volunteers.

This reversal of field would seem to be the leadership's true ministry to the individual member to help him see this call as a disciple under the Gospel. This gets the member away from playing the role merely of producer and the church leader as manager, and it places them both within their designated function in the body. The abilities and resources of people are to be discovered and developed through stewardship efforts. "As each has received a gift, employ it for one another, as good stewards of God's varied grace" (1 Peter 4:10 RSV). The Christian's eyes are directed to see his own abilities and blessings. Coiner declares: "God works through what He gives, and His gifts determine what the tasks of the Christian shall be." [8] This will keep churches from posing as judges of individuals who do not measure up to the pleas and standards of the organization *according to its needs,* for there is no way of truly measuring people and properly differentiating between them through such an approach. The proposed reversal of field will create a new image of stewardship and of the institution in the minds of members who have a warped conception of it.

One cannot fulfill his vocation by merely meeting an average or a specific church need, nor can he merely imitate other people, for no other person is his model, nor is the same activity and standard appropriate for everyone. Each priest of God is to concentrate on his own task. The church's program ought to encourage him to discover his own particular role.

Traditional practices in which leaders suggest financial goals to be met encourage a partial stewardship challenge. The power of the Holy Spirit is the power to carry the financial load, but only a few more dollars of an increased budget is the load proposed through many a stewardship effort. The approach gives a totally wrong impression of the responsibilities of God's priests in and to the church.

Rather, we see the Christian and his potential in the *total* responsibility of the covenant call. With the power of the Holy Spirit the load that love carries is seen in the spiritual gifts which God gives: mercy, generosity, witness, justice, service. Leaders are to teach and encourage people to accept more of each gift and grow more in each grace by the providence of God. This approach with its total challenge follows the theology of grace. There is a great difference between this scene and the other one where the impression is conveyed that the will of God is done through the successful carrying of a limited financial load determined by men (that may mean only 3 percent of their income) — while mercy for the downtrodden and love for the neighbor of another color and witness to the pagan friend is completely forgotten. *And these spiritual expressions of love*

111

are being neglected while budgets are being met and exceeded! Congregations can easily encourage a scene which in Luke 11:42 is condemned: "But woe unto you, Pharisees! for ye tithe mint and rue and all manner of herbs, and pass over judgment and the love of God; these ought ye to have done, and not to leave the other undone."

The task is much greater than adding a few more dollars to the church treasury each year. Many million dollars more will not do the job! If American churches would raise 500 million dollars more for world missions today, all of the evident world challenges would barely be touched. Latest estimates indicate that all Protestant missionaries in the world are annually reaching fewer than 2 million more non-Christians not already reached by all the mission stations in the world, while the yearly increase of world population is about 45 million people. The solution to this problem is more than acquiring an additional 500 million or even a billion dollars for world missions.

This is not to say that God is not calling for generous offerings from His people. Negative voices must be stilled which say that there are too many frills in the world program, or that the church is trying to advance too fast. There are the "little-love" disciples who want to "send them away" because they cry after us. However, it will only make matters worse to place the financial goal before these people. Whimpering and complaining will not be dispelled by human arguments and by organizational claims or by asking everyone to take on just a little more financial responsibility.

As financial needs become more demanding the primary purpose of the church and its ministries may be sidetracked. Religious convictions of members can easily be exploited to secure adequate support financially. Thus a congregation may seem to be more concerned with the man who is responsible for missing the budget than with the man who is hitting the bottle or his wife. This gives evidence of a detachment of stewardship and Christian giving from the purpose of the church as a whole. To establish the stewardship life on the basis of financial gifts to the church while ignoring the total ministry of each Christian is to ignore God's plan and to follow another Gospel — and as Paul told the Galatians, to establish a program of specific works is no Gospel at all. In essence such ways cover up signs of the church's failures and seek to redefine God's plan in little, manageable terms. At this rate the church does not come to the heart of true stewardship performance. A "separated piety" of stewardship may be maintained which ignores some of the vital features of the authentic priesthood and stewardship.

Many a church deems itself successful when all bills are paid and there is a balance in the treasury. God's holy name is often used to incite the congregation to meet a goal and to overcome the shortages occasioned by substandard giving habits. Meanwhile the hurt, the sick, and many without Christ all over all the world are passed by, while it is felt that the church has had a successful "stewardship" program.

Christian stewardship does not consist in raising money only, but in raising people together with their money. St. Paul puts it this way: "I seek not yours, but you" (2 Cor. 12:14). He was certainly indicating that the approach is to the whole man through the Word and was asking for much more than a financial response.

Money-raising is only part of a very broad picture — by itself it does much less for a congregation than most people think. It is apparent that St. Paul did not hesitate to gather money in the church; but his great stress was on motive, and his suggested method grew out of the motive. He showed that giving is a proposition of "hearts for God" rather than "purses for the church," of opening the heart through the Word rather than pinching the pocketbook through promotional pleas. As he gained the person by the preaching of the Gospel, Paul not only saw the purse included with the person but also other gifts as well. The heart of stewardship is the offering of the whole person.

Are members working *for* the church or *as* the church? Such admonitions as "Your church needs your help" and "Do something for your church today" only motivate laymen to think in terms of doing something *for* the church instead of being busy *as* the church. When we think of the church as God's agent of reconciliation, exhortative challenges as previously stated are quite dull and unimaginative. Our society is filled with institutions pleading for people's time, loyalty, and money. The church is not just another institution seeking the member's time and loyalty. Its work is not done only in its formal programs.

There is no such thing as stewardship devoid of social implications, for the theology of stewardship immediately confronts Christians with a number of vital matters other than giving of money for the church. Love for neighbors involves more than raising money to send a missionary to preach to them; it includes a personal interest in a broader way. A love that produces only limited financial fruits is no real love of neighbor. Even though members tithe, they have no justification for bypassing men in need.

As stewardship efforts go beyond institutional concerns they will guide members towards a consciousness of morality and civic righteousness which is imperative for their stewardship. Christian consciences should be aroused in such a way that they cause uneasiness in the midst of the perplexing and controversial moral problems of the community and world. Educational efforts ought to strengthen people so that they have the integrity of character to avoid moral cowardice and at the same time make their contribution as citizens in an era of indulgent and mad rushing for material wealth and social prestige. There is something tragically wrong if members continue to sit in pews every Sunday and bring their offerings faithfully — even serve the church in some way with their talents — but become preoccupied in their daily lives with unrecognized selfishness and greed and fail to make their voices heard in society. Gambling, political dishonesty, and other forms of vice and immorality in society will soon feel the force of Christian consciences that have been challenged by a true Biblical stewardship concept.

Stewardship efforts should seek to lay bare false pretenses of piety and to help people get away from the "averageness" and mediocrity that can never be a sufficient response to God. The task of stewardship efforts is not a ministry for the survival of the institutional church; God is allowing His people to survive for the greater ministry to which He is apparently calling them. The call to total mission may be muffled by equating a dollar challenge with God's total call.

Rules and Regulations Pervert the Group Ministry_

Healthy Christian growth is made difficult when leaders attempt to make rules that apply to all possible situations, thus narrowing in the congregation the range of the individual's choices and action. When leadership fails in its essential educational tasks, then the book of rules and regulations are placed in full view; then objectives are obscured by promotional thrusts and passing enthusiasms, and leaders become merely promoters.

Some leaders seem to feel that the proclamation of grace seems to leave too many loose ends, which can be quite irritating. Martin Marty writes: "Protestantism in its act of Reformation rejected the Law as the normative mode of regulating the Christian life. . . . The Law is not a ladder to heaven, a guidebook to interpret the merit badges of good Christian scouts." [9] The New Testament provides no rules under the covenant of grace but rather sets forth the principles which should guide the Christian. A distrust of the power of God's grace will tend to cause leaders to impose a system of discipline on others.

Devastating to the pursuit of the Christian calling is the tendency to complicate the simple Gospel of Jesus Christ and to make it say just a little more or less than it actually does, and to settle for dead formalism, empty traditionalism, or brittle intellectualism instead of being directed freely by the Spirit through the Word. Theodore Heimarck reminds, "Wittingly or unwittingly, cunningly attractive ways to enforce forms of voluntary servitude have been discovered by men who have massed to produce. . . . The assembly lines, the pressures of conformity, and the forces making man a consumer have all conspired to rob humanity of 'humanness.' . . . It would seem that this is hardly the moment for the church to forget her Lord's concern with the person, and that now, as never before, she ought to stand guard over the individual's right to be an individual as over against all institutions and organizations that seek to stifle the soul." [10]

The growth process and the law of love is submerged when men's criteria are brought into full view for the commitment. The intrusion of human suggestions can neutralize the power of Christ's love, for it centers attention on itself rather than on the motivating power of God. In reality the leaders seem to play God when they direct attention to the exact fruits they expect from people.

Werner Elert asserts, "We dare never lose sight of the fact that in our relationship with God grace and legal order are mutually exclusive." [11] Elert shows that much can be lost by not properly defining and understanding the nature of the Christian corporate community.[12] There are mutual responsibilities to each other, and leaders are responsible for ways in which an enriching fellowship may be maintained. The obedience of love does not mean subjection of one's will to others, but it does mean voluntary devotion and a willingness to listen to their proclamation.

When congregations equate God's judgment with their own and try to tell people specifically what fruit is needed in order to be "successful," they seem to tell members each move they should make. If this is done in finances and stewardship, then why not also in witnessing, human relations, and other matters that are just as vital? Then why not proceed further and tell them how to spend each dollar they earn? Reasonable Biblical goals in Christian education and sanctification should be held before individuals. Paul's epistles are replete with such suggestions and advice. It is to be remembered, however, that St. Paul's objective was not the achievement of institutional goals but the response of love to satisfy evident needs according to the call.

"The church is called to be the people of God, and the terms of the call are God's terms and not man's." [13] As each believer sees himself as a priest *of Christ,* he realizes that he is responsible, not to church leaders first, but to God Himself. If the believers are not led to measure their primary privilege *as God's people,* neither can they hope to measure their responsibility *to God and His church.* Leaders may get what they ask, but the church should get what the Lord asks. If people are measured by men's ideas, they tend to measure their efforts by men's potential. Pressing specific institutional needs upon people creates a serious conflict between church needs and family needs. Man's goals or stated needs dare not become the focal point of guilt or failure in the Christian calling.

Living under group standards and man's judgment affords little joy in the church, little freedom, little vision or sense of divine calling and purpose; there is little courage to risk all in the certainty of victory, little spontaneity, and little humor. Instead there is much intensity, pressure, artificiality, self-consciousness, fear of judgment and failure, self-justification, impression-making, and superficiality.

Members are servants and fools for Christ's sake, not for man's sake and to fulfill man's will. They are ministers *of Christ* and stewards of the mysteries *of God.* On that basis

St. Paul writes to the Christians at Corinth: "But with me it is a very small thing that I should be judged of you, or of man's judgment; yea, I judge not mine own self. For I know nothing by myself, yet am I not hereby justified; but he that judgeth me is the Lord. Therefore judge nothing before the time, until the Lord come, who both will bring to light the hidden things of darkness and will make manifest the counsels of the hearts; and then shall every man have praise of God." (1 Cor. 4:3-5)

Limited financial goals encourage *work righteousness* when followed to their logical conclusions, for "outsiders" must congratulate "insiders" for successful support, and "insiders" measure themselves by the standards of others. The old man likes rules and regulations and performance charts from outsiders. If they are too high, he has someone else to criticize; if they are low enough to reach, he can expect congratulations and gloat in his achievement. The Holy Spirit's voice can be stifled and muffled to the degree that men impose their own judgments and personal goals on others. God's Word leaves the way open for general goals and objectives, but in devised programs there is great concern about the setting of specific and predetermined standards and decisions for individuals at a particular time in the program.

Leaders and Members Can Be "Phonies" in This Ministry

"Make full proof of your ministry!" is said to pastors, but it must also be said to all Christians in their various ministries. There is a point when the true stewardship ministry is perverted. The covenant man is authorized only by Christ. As a stewardship leader he has nothing else to support his legitimacy but the message of the covenant Word.

The man who states: "I, a servant of God, declare unto you," should not become a deliveryman for stewardship promotional packets and for institutional goals that aim to meet human hopes. The church member who is to edify his fellow believer should not be forced to exchange his Bible for a church budget when he speaks to his fellow member about stewardship responsibilities. There is such a thing as switching roles unnecessarily and becoming spiritual "phonies."

No conscientious pastor should be expected to preach a stirring sermon on Sunday morning about the priesthood of all believers and then, after disrobing, become a salesman for the stated needs of the church. No church member should hear the clear call of God to the full ministry of reconciliation and then be handed a skeleton of a challenge in the form of a proposition which preaches man's judgment of man's performances. This forces a strange and tragic dichotomy of being and mission. The infinite relationship with Christ can be forced into a very finite relationship when authentic Christianity is transformed into a moralistic Christianity. This is done when promotional ideas are used to condition people to accept a limited church program as a substitute for the challenge to a full ministry. Then a sham situation is created that takes away the integrity of the spokesmen and their messages.

Whatever knowledge of stewardship realities may enter into man's vision from other sources, God's Word will confirm and complete what is of genuine worth. The conflict between Biblical concepts and the pressing needs of modern church life is not always apparent. There is always the possibility of subjective miscalculation and error. The life of love cannot be commanded. The New Testament does not have prophets, as the Old Testament did, who are God's spokesmen in such a way as to reveal what an exact task might be and what the cost is. Since God does not in His providence communicate His will for each specific situation to individuals in the form of specific decisions, stewardship leaders will take care that they do not assume this authority in the name of God.

The Group Expresses Its Stewardship Vocation
by Means of Financial Plans

There are three general stages or levels of giving that congregations may practice in their financial plans:

Stage 1. Needs are the measure for members' gifts.

Stage 2. Organizational concerns and suggestions dictate with a degree of flexibility the responsibilities of the members.

Stage 3. Personal values and priestly functions are the basic consideration in the Christian's decision of what he will give to his church.

These three stages are not necessarily mutually exclusive. "Personal values" and various "organizational needs" can both be proper elements which enter into some specific decisions. Our concern at this point is with the message employed to encourage givers to give.

A. *Avoid a Need-centered Approach*

Generally, most congregations have passed out of the inflexible No. 1 stage, need-centered giving. Most congregations have now adopted the more flexible second level, organization-centered giving. Some congegations are striving to work honestly and frankly at the third stage as they teach Christian giving at the person-oriented or priest-centered level. There are many who believe that they are at the third stage, but their messages and methods will not stand the test of the Word which reveals that they are still at the second stage of organizational concerns.

In giving to "needs" and "shares" and "quotas" various congregations have found for many years that left-over giving usually met the demands of a minimum budget set by groups which were often unknowingly defending their own billfolds. When giving was under consideration, people would be directed to the price tag of budgets or needs rather than to an emphasis *simply and purely on the act of giving as an expression of faith and love* which responds to

120

all needs. This in no way reflects on the faith of these leaders, but it does say that there was a definite lack of study and understanding of the theological implications of their messages for giving. During the past 30 to 40 years the church was blessed by the presence of some bright stewardship "lights" who wrote excellent Scriptural treatises on Christian giving, but it appears that congregations for the most part did not practice and little understood the fine concepts these men shared. In very recent years change has been much in evidence.

The church today has marched a long way and is earnestly seeking to get away from the "needs" approach. We have now come to the point in the organizational approach where more and more churches set "work programs" or use "program builders" instead of budgets and let the people face the opportunities seen by their leaders in the work program. Churches are also getting away from the inflexible gauge of "quotas" and "fair shares." This transition still finds leaders generally pointing members to considered opinions of financial goals and standards. It finds most churches at the point where stewardship, as in the past, is made simply a matter of giving to needs instead of managing all of the life for the ministry of reconciliation.

There are those who oversimplify the matter by saying: "Tell the people what is needed, and they will give." Financial problems cannot be worked out financially any more than moral conflicts can be worked out morally. The solution does not lie in recounting current church work as though it had the motivating power of the Scriptures. The Acts of the Apostles is the Word, but modern acts of the church are not. In such a stewardship approach churches have surrendered some of the distinctive traits that mark them as the church. So subtle is this invasion of moralism, pragmatism, and humanism in stewardship that it is very difficult to be aware of the inconsistency of the situation.

When God taught His people how to give, He did not

stress a motivation of the "needs" of the temple or of the Levites. God refers His people *to what He has given and to what they have*. When St. Paul told of a great need, he did not ask the Corinthian Christians to give according to a budget for the relief of the great need in Jerusalem; he simply said: "Give as God has given."

Imagine if Bill said to his wife, "I'm going to love you just as much as Tom loves his wife." Would she be flattered or satisfied? This is not the language of love. She wants Bill to love her with all his heart (capacity). Tom does not belong in the picture at all. In the same sense the appeal for acts of love in stewardship and giving do not come from what others are doing or what the "average" need may be.

Luther P. Powell writes: "As money-making becomes more necessary the spiritual leaders lose sight of the primary purpose of the church and their ministries. . . . They have exploited the religious convictions of man in order to support the institution." [14]

K. Kuntz declares: "The terrible limitation of giving to meet need rests in the fact that once a particular need is met, the giver has no larger motivation for his stewardship. . . . Giving to meet need is circumscribed by the ability of the donor to know the evident needs. In this sense, one's stewardship is never greater than the image of man. The result is to build a way of life which allows human knowledge to block the flow of mercy, love, and kindness." [15]

If God's love is the motivation for serving and giving, then this Gospel message should be used to motivate people. If God's Word is the power and guide for giving, then this Word should be used to empower and instruct people without confusing them by the use of organizational concerns. Spirituality and faith are raised by the Spirit through the Word and sacrament. It is theologically wrong to try to produce spiritual fruits and financial gifts by using financial needs as the magnet that pulls the response.

There are those who say that their "suggested askings" or

appeals for needs are brought only in the form of information and are suggested in an evangelical framework. Then it should be asked: "Is the suggested asking or specific financial need to be taken *seriously?*" If this is to be taken seriously, then the individual faces a new factor in his decision for one of the areas of his sanctified life. It cannot be said that theology does not apply in the matter because this is supposed to be a "practical matter." There is no double standard for theory and practice; when a person talks of "practical efforts," he does not switch theological principles. Dietrich Ritschl writes, "Legitimate practice in the church is not only connected with theology; it is theology." [16] This fact is vital to everything stated in stewardship messages.

Some assume that a "suggested asking" or a similar directive assures proper decisions and that a lack of some directive is inviting irresponsibility. This is a false assumption, for it denies the effective processes of grace. Action under grace should heighten the feeling of responsibility since the focus becomes even more pointed at God's will and love rather than a focus on man's financial appraisal of God's will. Giving money really has very little to do with what is in one's wallet but has much to do with grace. Many people will trust God if they have a bank balance, and so they will respond to the need. But faith and trust are to be built up; the task is not one of reminding people how big their bank balance is.

Roy Smith once wrote: "The visit of the kings was an occasion of such joy that even the most extravagant gifts were not considered a burden. No one worried about a 'quota' or about 'doing one's share.' Imagine, if you can, what a sordid thing the visit would have been if the three kings had stopped to calculate their respective responsibilities and made it all a matter of careful bookkeeping. Instead, each one prepared his gift as the outpouring of his heart."

Christians, both strong and weak, must become confused

when they are the object of repeated annual appeals for reaching local and world mission budgets, for periodic building funds, for new equipment funds, and for pet projects or regular emergencies. Some programs are only thinly veiled to hide the "fruit-plucking" intentions behind them. Rather the church needs to concern itself with intensive training, or as Jesus calls it in Luke 13:8: "digging and dunging." Men can stand under the fig tree and plead that they need the fruit, but only when they dig and dung and prune will there be adequate motivation for response to the evident need. The "digging and dunging" task is the major responsibility of church leaders, while "fruit-plucking" is incidental to the educational phase. God says: "Every tree is known by his own fruit" (Luke 6:44). God measures fruit by what *He* has *given*, not by what *we* might *expect*. In the parable Jesus indicates that the duty of the churchman is to cultivate and fertilize, to be interested in the health of the member.

Needs are usually computed by a budget. Arthur McKay asserts: "When a church budget is determined primarily, maybe even entirely, by carefully computing how much the members can be expected to increase their annual pledges, when it is subsequently presented in ways that call upon the members to share equally in underwriting it, when the focus is on 'average' and 'fair-share' gifts, the opportunity to encourage genuine proportionate giving is lost." [17] Many a congregation tries desperately both to motivate by the budget and encourage proportionate giving. Some will assert that "giving is not a matter of budgets or programs" but then proceed to select Bible stories as motivation to present together with their stated needs. Or they will expect financial growth in the church more for economic reasons (greater financial ability) than for reasons of faith.

"Budgetitis" haunts many congregations more than they care to admit. Various pastors and congregations have refused to undertake a thorough program of training in giving and a program of ongoing mission education because they "always make the budget" and reach their "fair share"— besides, "prices and crops are good so there is no problem of raising money." As this book was being prepared, continuing evidence was seen. A January Sunday church bulletin spoke of the significance of making a budget: "OUR GOAL REACHED — Yes, folks! You did it again! This proves beyond a shadow of a doubt that you are God's people and that you desire to promote His cause." Do attained financial goals prove that the people responsible for the attainment are God's people? Group loyalty and church pride have achieved some "good" financial records in the past; present demands are stretching that loyalty to the breaking point in many lives.

The budget approach has caused many problems and has opened many questionable paths of approach in message and method. We have seldom seen such elation as when a group for the first time in the ninth month reached and even exceeded by a few dollars the *monthly* requirements based on the budget — and this is called a rare accomplishment which should bring special joy to every concerned Christian! Or another leader writes: "If it were possible to add *just one more month* to the current fiscal year, we should not find it too difficult to meet our budget" — how can we believe that thirteen months in one year would settle financial problems? Or when the monthly receipts for one entire year were listed in a column, the writer stated: "Note especially the figures for December. All glory to God!" December and the gifts some people brought that month may look terrible in relation to the total offerings and the percentage they gave to their Lord for one year — yet under the budget approach December receipts become a matter of great elation. (While their lives may lack love and mercy, are we to give glory to God?)

The financial plea of a church in a large city was settled by this statement in one of its folders: "Could you *spare* 25 cents more per week, a quarter over last year's contributions?" What about the situation where members complain about the increased budget, but they are reminded over and over again by leaders that *Jesus* is asking. We seriously question whether Jesus is asking that specific sum and whether the motivation of His love can be tied so completely to any specific annual budget. The giving challenge does not lie in the request for people to add 10 percent to last year's pledge or to add 50 cents a week over last year's giving. It is also quite dismaying to see that the great themes of various high festivals of the church are often used as motivational schemes to raise a budget that is in the red.

The *annual* battle of the budget is arbitrary and unnatural. This matter is one of a *life* battle of spiritual habits; the issue is one of an ongoing crusade of firstfruit, generous proportionate giving. To use "wedges" for financial hopes is an expediency and tends to produce artificial fruit or possible unwilling offerings or ones in which the givers glorify the gift as the work of their own righteousness.

We do not rule out special appeals, properly conceived and properly constructed. However, subtle twists can be easily made. For example, leaders can see a great need for a larger sum this year. Therefore the emphasis of the Gospel must be stepped up — and at once there is the danger of making the Gospel a "gimmick" to meet that special budget.

The budget is usually a compromise between the positively and the negatively thinking members, between the optimistic and the pessimistic. Many budget allotments, especially for world missions, have allowed only second-rate efforts for first-rate causes. *Budgets have been expressive only of hoped-for performances rather than of admitted responsibility.*

There are stewardship programs that seem to be a "selling" of the church. The church has nothing to sell, only a message to proclaim: the Gospel of Jesus Christ. Paul's epistles do not try to sell the Ephesians on their own congregation, or on the grand Pauline Conference of Churches, or even on the United Church of Asia Minor, or any other group, but simply let them face the Gospel and the importance of repentance and forgiveness, worship, education, preaching, fellowship, and welfare.

Could you imagine St. Paul recasting 1 Cor. 16:2 into a message for organizational goals and writing: "Now concerning the collection, let everyone give generously and meet the Corinthian budget of 2,480 shekels, and let everyone give his share so that this budget might be met." Even amidst a particular need that dealt with only a specific number of Jerusalem saints, he indicated no organizational goal but faced each member of the congregation with the "individual goal" of giving as God has given to him.

What should a person make of the motivational factor if he moves from an area which has world mission requirements that average at $25 to an area where the average is $40 (arbitrarily set to guide people to give, not reflecting *actual* needs)? Or say that he moves from a congregation whose average total "needs" are $170 per member — why should he change giving habits simply because of his change of residence and therefore faces a different budget? Is it that God's love for him has changed or are the stated needs the motivation? Or let's say that the change is in reverse — since "needs" has been the big cry and plea for additional funds, is he now to cut back because the cry is not so insistent and so high? If budgets are to be the measure of offerings, then it would seem that members are justified in shopping around for congregations in their area with the smallest budget and then transfer to that congregation.

A personal experience might be valuable to recount. In a 4-year period in two cities of residence our family did not know what the budgets of our own congregations were since the congregations did not advertise them and the author was out of the city every fall on the nights when the budgets were set. Three questions arise: Did God's love for our family change simply because we did not know what the budget was? Should our love for God have changed because we did not know what the budget was? If giving is an expression of love and faith, then should the lack of knowledge of the budget have any effect on our giving?

There may be very logical reasons behind the procedure of setting a budget and asking people to pledge towards it, but some dangerous elements are brought with the procedure. The budget, originally intended to be a *tool* in the service of Christian stewards, gradually but very forcefully became the *"god"* that demanded payment to meet its ends. By raising the means or the tool (budget) to the status of an end or objective, the church has unwittingly deprived itself of the power to fulfill its many and increasing stewardship responsibilities. The budget does not have the ability to move self-centered people to give anything. Aside from causing resentment because it faces people with cold figures, the budget that was designed to be a helper has become an enemy. And what is worse, anyone who associates himself with the budget, whether it be pastor, treasurer, or stewardship committee, becomes an enemy of the people, too.

Someone asks about the Good Samaritan who saw the needs as he viewed the needy brother and opened his heart in compassion to him; but what about the priest and Levite who saw the same blood flowing from the man's body? The difference was obviously the way in which each had been previously motivated. One doesn't stand next to the priest or Levite and tell them: "You see the man hurt by the roadside, help him." These men had enough laws and enough knowledge, but they lacked love which comes from proper motivation. There are many who act more like the priest and Levite than the Good Samaritan, and they will not be motivated by further exposition of the financial needs but rather they will be moved only by the power of the Word and the Spirit.

Only after people have the proper understanding and motivation does Jesus encourage, saying: "Open your eyes and see the fields ready for the harvest." There is a great difference between the *general* needs ("the fields are white") and man's *stated* or *calculated* needs (the "work program" or "budget"). The *general* need of the vast harvest that is being lost is part of the general reason for giving sacrificially; the *second* need (man's financial calculation) is but the occasion for the gift and for the division of the gift. People who are like the priest and Levite will not be inspired beyond the giving of a few more dollars when the budget or work program is proclaimed in inspiring terms. Rather, the Scriptural way is the use of the Word that shows members their relationship and response to Christ even while leaders show the *general* need to which Christian love must respond. As people's eyes of faith are opened to God's goals for them, their eyes of love will open to human needs.

The British writer Brian Rice urges his readers: *"Don't go to your people with a budget. . . .* Should congregations be trained to give without reference to a target? This whole discussion is based on the affirmative, but some find this difficult to accept. I think of Christian giving as a spiritual practice similar to prayer." [18]

The place that a budget should assume is answered in the timing; it is a question of *when* it is to be introduced to the membership. The budget is not to be used to fill the treasury but rather to empty it. The budget should be set only after all pledges have been made, and then it should be used only as a spending guide, not a guide for giving. It is the tool by which offerings are apportioned for God's work, and it establishes a sequence of priorities. It informs the treasurer how to spend. It really has no other purpose. When the spending guide has been set, the congregation must be willing to live with the consequences and not panic in the tenth or eleventh month when a shortage may loom large. This is the time to keep faith with the people, relying only on a Gospel reminder of God's continued acts of mercy and love.

B. *Set Budgets After the Group Presents the Message*

A growing number of congregations are conducting their teaching efforts before setting their budget. The Presbyterian Church in the U. S. has been urging a "prebudget" educational program for some years already and attests to the blessings of this approach.

The "prebudget" Every Member Stewardship Visit means that the educational program is conducted before the budget is presented or adopted. If the budget has been adopted, it is to be kept *totally* in the background until the pledge effort has been concluded. This will help put the emphasis in the right place: giving to God rather than underwriting a budget.

The "prebudget" Every Member Stewardship Visit brings great spiritual blessings — also assuring financial increases. It is not some new "gimmick" for raising money; there are no tricks in this approach. It is an educational approach with true integrity. It avoids being a 1-year financial project. It confronts the individual with his responsibilities to God without reference to *calculated* needs for motivation.

This approach is designed to tell the members of each congregation: "God's priests, it's up to you! By your offerings and pledges you are setting the total work your church will do." How many times have members said: "If only I could set the budget of our church. . . !" In the prebudget effort they really do help set the total budget of the congregation, although leaders must do the work of establishing the financial priorities when the pledges are known. Thus the members' faith and vision determine the ministry and outreach of their church.

A Nebraska pastor utilizing this educational emphasis states: "This type of grace system is proper, for it puts the burden of the decision on the individual where it belongs. If we can warm the people more to the *general* needs and the *overall* white harvest, the results will be there without the stating of needs in dollars and cents. This approach encourages the individual Christian to do some personal thinking about what the church wants. It takes continual and persistent education through the Gospel, but it's the one way which allows the Holy Spirit full room to operate. We are beginning to believe and act as a dynamic organism, and the facade of our religious pretenses is beginning to crumble as the individual's responsibility is seen toward the Word and directly related to God's love in Christ instead of responsibility to the immediate financial requests of the church."

A pastor from a midwest city recently wrote: "Is there fear that the Kingdom will suffer if we remove the crutch of financial goals? I think such a fear is quite unjustified and results are exactly the opposite. My fear is that the Kingdom may be suffering now because we have gotten into God's way with our plans, although our intentions were of the highest sort. Should we be willing to postpone the day of light and grace while we limp along on a crutch and the Kingdom suffers? That's why I say, *go all the way!* I insist that the Bible places my giving in the area of 'my personal worship of God.' Since this is true for me, the congregation has no more right to pass resolutions that control my giving than they do to pass resolutions about how loud I sing or how long my prayers should be."

In order to prevent frequent building fund efforts in a growing congregation, it is well to include anticipated building projects in the regular budgets. Because of the enlarged vision and greater income gained in the education program in proportionate giving, the congregation may expect increased income year by year. This increased income will allow the congregation to set aside a good amount annually for its anticipated building needs and thus reduce the need of a heavy debt and of a big campaign when building becomes a necessity. This is another blessing of the prebudget Every Member Stewardship Visit.

C. *"Needs" Properly Portrayed Through Mission Information*

The confusion in the use of needs comes from a lack of definition of needs and what their proper use is in motivation. The whole point of Christian love is a response to need and needs. Jesus came to heal the sick and to forgive sinners because "the sick need a physician." God's people should have adequate information about the work they are doing through their offerings. They have a ministry that responds to need, but it is an issue of why, how, and when to present these needs to them.

The epistles show that St. Paul was regularly telling the people about the progress and the problems of the church work he was doing. His stewardship and mission education program was one of reminding God's people how God was blessing the work, or of indicating problems for which they needed to pray: "Things which happened unto me have fallen out rather unto the furtherance of the Gospel" (Phil. 1:12). He told them about evidences of God's grace at work: "When they were come and had gathered the church together, they rehearsed all that God had done with them, and how He had opened the door of faith unto the Gentiles." (Acts 14:27)

People are benefited by mission information because it helps them understand the general need for greater mission activity. They should learn of the plight of the heathen and also of the way in which the church is reaching them. They should hear the full truth of the mission situation in the world and of the unending tasks they face. People have a right to know what is happeneing with their offerings, how others are helped, and also how the church is failing to reach out.

While mission information is not a motivation for giving and is not a substitute for God's Word, it is required so that the Christian and the congregation may have an indication how to *divide* offerings properly between the great causes of the church locally and worldwide. People should know and understand that processes are at work to provide for all spiritual enterprises to which the response of love can and should be made. Mission information is a report, not a motivation.

The church does not lack for adequate and effective tools for mission education. Most church bodies have supplied sufficient mission study folders, mission news through their denominational magazines, filmstrips, and motion pictures. These excellent tools are worthless unless they are used properly. Aside from portraying God's grace in Christ clearly in all preaching, teaching, and the faithful use of the Word and sacraments, good mission education involves regular mission quotes in bulletins, altar prayers, mission stories in Sunday school, a mission library, mission applications and stories in sermons regularly, bulletin inserts available from the denominational headquarters, visual aids, special mission fairs and mission Sundays, and short mission talks at organizational meetings. It involves regular opportunities to give to world missions, and also assurances to people that their mission offerings are sent to their designated place without delay.

Notes for Chapter 6

[1] Harry G. Coiner, "The Secret of God's Plan," *Concordia Theological Monthly,* XXXIV, No. 5 (May 1963), 268.

[2] Richard Byfield and James P. Shaw, *Your Money and Your God* (Garden City, N. Y.: Doubleday & Co., Inc., 1959), pp. 55, 56.

[3] The author has sought to provide direction to congregations for dealing with fruitless lives and inactive members in his book *Winning Them Back* (Minneapolis: Augsburg Publishing House, 1963).

[4] Kenneth Kuntz, *Wooden Chalices* (St. Louis: Bethany Press, 1963), pp. 138, 139.

[5] M. H. Grumm, "Motivation in Paul's Epistles," *Concordia Theological Monthly,* XXXV, No. 4 (April 1964), 217.

[6] Pastors will derive benefit from reading John E. Herrmann's *The Chief Steward* (St. Louis: The Lutheran Church — Missouri Synod, 1951). While this manual for pastoral leadership was written specifically for the author's own denomination, it is pertinent reading for all Protestant pastors.

[7] Some of the thoughts of the preceding six paragraphs were taken from notes on a presentation by Martin L. Koehneke on "The Teaching Role of the Stewardship Leader," Dec. 13, 1963.

[8] Coiner, p. 270.

[9] Martin E. Marty, *The Hidden Discipline* (St. Louis: Concordia, 1962), p. ix.

[10] Theodore Heimarck, *Preaching for the Tethered Man* (Minneapolis: Augsburg, 1962), pp. 68, 69.

[11] Werner Elert, *The Christian Ethos,* trans. Carl J. Schindler (Philadelphia: Muhlenberg Press, 1957), p. 208.

[12] Elert, p. 337.

[13] Rachel Henderlite, *Forgiveness and Hope* (Richmond: John Knox Press, 1961), p. 119.

[14] Luther P. Powell, *Money and the Church* (New York: Association Press, 1962), p. 64.

[15] Kuntz, p. 85.

[16] Dietrich Ritschl, *A Theology of Proclamation* (Richmond: John Knox Press, 1960), p. 7.

[17] Arthur McKay, *Servants and Stewards* (Philadelphia: Geneva Press, 1963), p. 25.

[18] Brian Rice, *What Is Christian Giving?* (London: SCM Press, 1958), p. 67.

Chapter 7

Stewardship Ministry Through Organization and Forms

What forms are best suited to the stewardship ministry? Who is the person to be reached? What are the problems and obstacles in reaching him? What methods will then aid in reaching all people?

The tendency is toward mastery through forms, whereas forms should be a marvelous servant of people. Forms and organization are useful as long as they serve the Christian vocation under the covenant Gospel. The group ministry does not take place in a formless vacuum.

Organization and Form in Stewardship Activities

The title of this book indicates the unity and flow of theology, message, and method in stewardship considerations. Method and forms become considerations only after Biblical theology and message have been learned. Message is conveyed through organization and methods. If there is to be existence of any good thing, there must be form. When food is placed on the table, good organization and methods helped get it there. Only a fanatic would desire to dissolve organization and method or even contend against it. Method is like packing things in a box; a good packer will get in much more than a bad one. Methods are not a necessary evil, but a necessary virtue. The Word of God leads to the work of God — the Word *and work* go together.

The big question is what kinds of forms will be acceptable to perform the church's tasks. Methods are designed as a means for functioning according to the Christian calling and as a means of serving people. Since the church is a dynamic phenomenon there should be constant searching for new ways and new expressions of doing the work.

The humanistic approach that uses existing forms as the beginning point for the stewardship task leads the church astray, for it invariably accommodates the Word to suit the notions of the members. Structured programs (forms) can stifle grace in narrow bounds so that the message of the Word is distorted. Christ is the real point of beginning, and the Word is the expression of His will.

The church's unique quality is that it is able to effect necessary change without revolution. But this demands a consciousness of the relation of existing form to function, a realization of how the Word is conveyed by channels. A decisive feature of the church is that it must ever be ready to overthrow idols of forms which may invade its territory. No form or method should be disturbed irresponsibly or accepted without close scrutiny. Theology is not "anti-institutional," but rather it helps put function and form into proper perspective and finds the place of the institution in the message.

Eduard Schweizer writes: "Church order is to be regarded as a part of the proclamation in which the church's witness is expressed, as it is in its preaching. . . . Certainly the church that lacks order does not cease to be a church, but its service is impaired. . . . When we ask about the church's order, we must also try to understand the church's essential nature." [1] People often allow the institutional forms to become ends in themselves, and when this happens their loyalty as God's people is judged by their service to the church in the specific program and form.

There is certainly nothing wrong in wanting to preserve a certain type of organization and method, but there must be good reason for it. Some forms, also in stewardship, grew out of specific needs but were never thoughtfully studied. From their experiences, some leaders absolutized the stewardship messages and methods of the past and thus lost some of the Biblical perspective. Such people have assumed that *their response* to the Word was in essence His stewardship Word to them — thus experience became a substitute for the Word and dictated stewardship action.

Well-meaning leaders are tempted to depend upon organization and form in the place of dialog and message in order to speed up matters, and so the spiritual inwardness and the contact with the individual as an individual becomes less evident. The character of the organization (and of the individual) is always harmed when ideals are sacrificed on the altar of success and conformity. Through demands to follow form blindly the institution exhausts its members and forces them into compulsive behavior and almost forces them to be neurotic extroverts. Because the people themselves know nothing else, they tend to identify their institutional stewardship experiences and form with authentic Christianity and do not realize it when their priesthood has become institutionalized. They become so much a part of the organization that it is hard to unwind, and it is also a question of whether they can afford to or not.

"Organization never goes deep enough to make or transfigure the deepest dimensions of man's life. . . . We organize things when we fail to redeem them. . . . Many churches can organize 3,000 people without changing any of them. Organization is a speedy way of deceiving ourselves into thinking that we have done something. . . . I'm not saying that we can do without organization. . . . But there are ways by which we men are able to organize far beyond the point of sustaining life, and many of our organizational enthusiasms actually exhaust life." [2]

How many people are possibly baffled, almost crushed, by the stultified institutionalism of some church programs? The "mass" approach, the rigid manuals, and the organizational claims upon them are a part of the agony and the bewilderment some members experience. We can find situations where the stewardship program itself had been so identified with divine sanction, where people had been so legalistically herded by institutional goals, that well-meaning people came to believe that they were disagreeing with God if they did not gladly follow the specific program and its propositions. So brash have been some stewardship efforts and so rigid their forms! There comes a time when the form and the method become the substitute for the function and where they exhaust the energy of many people while the task is doing little to change them or make life more meaningful for them. There is a dictatorship of forms which should be recognized for the legalistic conformity that it is in fact.

The problem is well defined by Bruce Reinhart in his excellent book *The Institutional Nature of Adult Christian Education*. Reinhart states: "The integrity of the institution is endangered through an unconscious drift into uncompromising discrepancies between theological definitions of purpose and their functional embodiment. . . . Certain operating pressures of the religious institution inevitably have their own influence upon the educational program of the church. In brief, what is taking place is that the educational program of the church is adapting to the wishes and needs of the organization as a whole." [3]

It is because of the battle between the old nature and new nature that this problem of institutionalism, forms, and methods exists. The flesh asks what authority the institution has, and what power. The new nature asks what opportunities and tasks it should perform. The old nature makes an idol of the form which offers security and conformity while the new nature wants to express its strength in freedom. The old nature accepts an idolatry which refuses God's plan for believers, for the old man wants to determine for himself how he is related to God. The new nature sees the Holy Spirit shattering wrongful human forms and ways by which men live and stake their success. When the Holy Spirit is heeded through the Word, the Christian life and congregational activity will not be reduced to sheer formalism which asks: "How did we do it last year? What success did we have and how much dare we hope for now?"

The institutional church needs to remember the diversity that exists in the unity of the body through the priesthood and to encourage the expression of this diversity instead of demanding blind conformity. The church will do well to idealize this diversity and speak of the great number of stewardship possibilities under grace. Church government and forms are something members need, but not at the expense of diversity. The church must not be a party to a divisive and inadequate loyalty.

The Form or Method for Ministry Carries a Vital Load

When spiritual functions are left to themselves without guidance and left to be done spontaneously without organization, there will not necessarily be a forming of a proper mode of expression. If Christian love does not take form, either corporately or individually, it is abstract and lacks practical worth. Even the deepest life of love needs simple form and direction if it is to be channeled effectively to the points of need. While our theology does not present a specific course of action, it does demand action. Carelessness and timidity also are unfaithfulness to our Lord. The one who has church responsibilities and keeps silent about God's claim upon men delivers them to a false life, false hopes, and false lords.

Some do not adopt a necessary method or form simply because they have not yet understood the function and the message. They are confused and stymied because they do not understand the nature of the task. This indicates why the pastors of a certain area refused to believe that there were any benefits in the EMSV [Every Member Stewardship Visit]: they did not want the EMSV because they said that they "just don't operate on a 'shot in the arm.'" They said: "We teach proportionate giving in our pulpits as much as possible. But we want you to understand we are not denying our laymen a thing." Of course, blindly they were denying their laymen a vital ministry in edifying one another and in performing their stewardship teaching function in the congregations. The fact is that the pastors were not teaching proportionate giving either! Their lack of program was a shameful abuse of the lay resources God had given to the church.

Soundly Biblical messages and effective methods should go together. Pious phrases and blind faith will not administer or finance the Kingdom. Ours is a God of order and method. Some pastors and leaders have an aversion to structured programs and offer no effective activity to accomplish what needs to be done. Some reject new structured forms, even though the obvious void is not filled by an adequate substitute. Leaders must sometimes share the blame for this organizational vacuum because of an inflexible authority that forces a guided take-this-or-take-nothing program on people. Acceptance of the guided program is not the problem at the moment, but the problem is the failure to understand the function of the activity to be pursued. This is the reason why there are congregations that refuse to have stewardship committees and why others will not conduct EMSV's.

A Detroit layman expressed himself on the importance of effective methods in these thoughts: "I think we must concede a victory to Satan, who for generations now has kept us sold on the idea that this matter of Christian sacrificial giving dare only be dealt with in abstract terms. And, because many people are inclined to take offense at the subject, we dare not personally confront one another. I am grateful to God that in the past I was subjected to some of these messages *by personal confrontation* (EMSV), and for the first time in my life I learned the joy of proportionate giving. Having heard the needs of the church expounded in eloquent form for 30 years, I was down there in the lower two thirds, among the 'niggardly' givers. And I figured that I was doing all or more than my share. Somehow the message never got through to me, nor to most of my fellow members."

Method is vital in the transmission of a lively stewardship and giving message. St. Paul apparently believed in going beyond a general proclamation of the stewardship and giving message. He had in the instance of the Corinthians stated the case of Christian giving in classic terms. Yet he sent men out to make sure that the people were properly cultivated and prepared (2 Cor. 9:3) — a specific effort at confrontation.

Because it used methods wrongly to assure success, the church has not always found itself able to minister to its people as effectively as it should. Message and method easily become introverted. A congregation can finally get to the point where its stewardship program is no longer an act of edifying and training membership for discipleship, but the program becomes a means of managing the church to achieve its aims and goals.

When one analyzes stewardship devices, methods, and crisis approaches of the past and present he will drop some of them for one of the following reasons: 1) They are being used as a quick expedient to overcome or bypass a weakness in individual Christians; or 2) They have no foundation or authority in the Scripture; or 3) They do not reach the basic cause of the problem, the inadequate level of individual sanctification. When everything external is stripped off in stewardship and one gets down to the core of the problem, the answer is simple: *The growth and development of God's priests according to the Biblical educational process is based on the Gospel of forgiveness.*

Robert E. Coleman reminds that "men were Jesus's method." In order to get the job done, Jesus wraps a man around the message. Coleman writes: "It all started by

Jesus calling a few men to follow Him. . . . His concern was not with programs to reach the multitudes, but with men whom the multitudes would follow. . . . He did not let His method obscure His lesson. He let His truth call attention to itself, and not the presentation. . . . This may be hard to imagine in this day of professional techniques and sure-fire gimmicks."[4]

Whether methods are successful or not is not the problem at this moment. In fact it may be wonderful when methods are successful, and it is not necessarily damaging when certain ones do achieve high success and popularity. The fundamental test of form and method and program is whether it is accomplishing the spiritual purpose which God calls for.

Stereotyped and inflexible messages and methods, used over and over again with only changes of titles and names, become wearisome and futile. Paul Lindemann almost 40 years ago pointed out some of the organizational inconsistencies in Christian giving when he said: "Systematization is not stewardship. . . . The contention has been made that the dearth of funds necessary to carry on our work successfully was due to the lack of proper machinery. . . . We have preached systematization with laudable persistence. . . . We have furnished reams of statistics. We have sought to set the official machinery of our [church body] into operation in an effort to introduce effective methods of collecting the gifts for the Kingdom of God. . . . Why is it that the earnestly applied remedies of systematizing our finances and of educating [i.e., church *information*] our people have not brought the expected and desired results?

"Christian giving needs a *heart stimulus*. It is animated not by a logic and reason and church patriotism and pride of achievement or even by a sense of duty, but its *actuating impulse* must be love. The most meticulous systematization and the most thorough and factual educa-

142

tion can never stimulate love. . . . A church may be thoroughly informed regarding the various church endeavors. It may have a complete picture of the church's missionary program. It may be thoroughly conversant with detailed tabulations of the church's financial needs. And yet the individual church member finds it difficult to realize that these needs have any relationship to him personally. . . . Something must be done to perfect a more adequate program of training in stewardship principles. . . . It stands to reason that only after the principles of stewardship have been recognized, the education along the facts of church needs and the institution of a system will bear the desired results. . . . It is high time that we come to our people boldly, asking not for a congregational and personal handout of the driblets of what they have left after they have satisfied all their own personal needs and luxuries, but that we come to them with the philosophy of life which the Holy Scriptures proclaim as the only logical reason why God has given us life. . . . It seems to us that what we need is a persistent, continuous campaign of stewardship education, not a six week's or a six month's or even a six year's effort, but the patient inculcation of stewardship principles." [5] What a penetrating analysis and solution!

To arrive at the method that best fits its theology and purpose, the congregation through its leaders should define its problems, seek reasonable solutions, and then organize intelligently for the educational task through which members are trained to make responsible decisions.

Give Attention to Educational Forms

Some seem to think that they can expect good fruit from a sick tree and that good stewardship habits automatically accompany belief in Jesus. Far too many have administered the stewardship affairs of their congregation as though poor Christians could and were willing to serve faithfully and practice good giving habits. By exhortations they expect weak members to serve and give generous offerings.

Rice states: "The outstanding problem in so many parishes is *not* that people do not give, but that they are not *trained* to give! . . . *People give, not as they are able, but as they understand!"* [6]

The Lord Jesus did not say: "Go ye and collect money so that missionaries can go into all the world!" but He did say: "Go ye into all the world, make disciples and TEACH!"

A proper educational approach should create new stewardship concepts in the members. Rice writes: "Where a congregation is being taught to give, the parish church will be developing the proper natural resources with which to spread the Gospel." [7] That congregation will find leaders through the EMSV playing the role of Christian witnesses to Scriptural truths, not beggars or raisers of budgets.

The church and each Christian is a field under cultivation. Phillips' version of 1 Cor. 3:9 is: "You are a field under God's cultivation." Christians and congregations are not finished products like a field whose grain has fully ripened and is ready for harvest. If a Christian or a congregation were a finished product, a fully ripened field, they would not need the workers they have — the tillers, planters, waterers — with their program of education, stewardship, and evangelism.

If the seed is to sprout, grow, and be fruitful, then rocks, weeds, and stumps must first be removed. Ground that has been plowed up and then ignored and left for the sun to harden and for the rain to pack, will never be fruitful ground. "Break up your fallow ground," God suggests (Hos. 10:12). Soil must be enriched by proper care. Seed is to be properly sown and watered. Everything in the field depends upon God's mercies and the response of the seed to those mercies. All the toil, preparation, and effort are expended to provide for the seed a suitable environment for its growth.

All of life is a sowing season. The whole work of the church is the story of the sower who went out to sow. Pastors, teachers, and leaders are called to give a full measure of devotion to the cultivation plan. They must go the whole way, from seedtime to harvest! The old nature would like to have half-seasons, but there is just no place for workers who watch the clock or who want half a season so that they can lounge on "Florida beaches" the rest of the time. The church will not gain any worthy advance by shortcuts, magic formulas, crash programs, clever publicity, smart promotional schemes, or just plain gimmicks. The laws of nature and the laws of the spiritual life will soon reveal both the careless and lazy sower.

Good stewardship commitment is part of the growth process, and effective educational forms help produce this. The vitality and genuiness of Christian faith become visible in a person's daily life and acts of commitment. Leaders owe it to every member to feed that faith with solid food before it is challenged to express itself in specific stewardship acts, especially in proportionate giving. They have to grapple with the theological issues that lie behind decisions and commitments. A superficial, moralistic approach will prove increasingly futile as the years pass by.

Stewardship education should provide solid informational material and not just inspirational stories or exhortations. Some leaders tell inspirational stories that inspire only. They only stir emotions but do not supply such education as will stir the will. In such a situation people cool off in a hurry and have no change of habit. Such exhortations as the following are very thin: "Let's all give more next year!" "Let's all consider tithing!" "Let's all march forward!" "If only more members would give sacrificially!" "All do more in '64!" "Let's all strive in '65!" Mere exhortations are weak because they do nothing to teach or inform. People usually know that what they are encouraged to do is good, but they feel powerless to act.

Exhorting them to do what they know they ought to do does not really help them.

Repeated exhortations tend to deaden people's consciences or to irritate them. What they need is *information* that exposes the problems and solutions of their dilemma. Information is meat while inspiration and exhortations are adrenalin. The meat gets into the sinews of the body while adrenalin only stimulates temporarily.

Because people give according to their knowledge and faith, not according to their ability, a sound educational form or program is the only answer. Each step of education has its own contribution to make towards achieving new and better giving habits. There are many cultivation opportunities and educational responsibilities for giving what Scripture teaches:

1. In the worship service sermons should be preached that truly convey a message from God, and laymen should supply "Minute-Men" talks that do the same. There should be special prayers and regular bulletin announcements and stewardship quotes.

2. The Sunday school and Bible class should be used for lessons on Christian giving.

3. The church organizations, men's and women's and youth,[8] should have a lively topic on the subject so that people might strengthen one another.

4. The home should receive a series of letters and tracts and a visit in order to study and learn these Scriptural truths.

5. The entire congregation should be reached through group meetings at the church or visits in every home.

Too often leaders have been satisfied with a pastoral sermon on the subject, with the thought that thus they have trained the parish in giving. We do not infer that the sermon is ineffective. The problem is this: Little coverage can be given in 20 to 30 minutes; many people who need to hear the message are absent; conditions are not conducive to such a challenge (some may be tired, some may be bothered by noise from children, some are not attentive; for others it is too hot and stuffy in the sanctuary); people generally are not ready for such a challenge in a sermon calling for the rather violent change in habits involved in proportionate giving. A more comprehensive form of education is required.

Ministering Through Organized Group Meetings

A concentrated educational program in Christian giving and stewardship can be conducted by using the following methods to reach all the members with the message: (1) The traditional way, an EMSV, calling at all homes; (2) Group meetings at the church or cottage meetings in homes, inviting people in different groups to come and hear and discuss the message of stewardship. It is a mistake to believe that the only or best way to present the stewardship message is through a visit in the home. Group meetings at church are sometimes much more effective than a short visit in the home because such meetings allow more time for education.

For a variation some congregations have experienced great blessings by conducting *group meetings at the church*. The members are divided into four, five, or six groups, one group being invited at one time to one of the meetings held at the church during one week. Those who are absent are then visited in their homes. We would urge everyone to consider this an excellent variation of the EMSV.

Good attendance is assured by adequate publicity, individual invitation by letter, and telephone reminders. Visitors are needed to make calls on those who are absent from these meetings. Absentees should be called by telephone the next morning in order to invite them to one of the remaining meetings. Meetings might be held every

147

night during one of the weeks in November, and a follow-up meeting might be held for all absentees several days later before the visitors go out and call on absentees.

The program and message for the group meetings at church might include: (1) Scripture reading — Matt. 6:24-33; prayer; (2) film: "The Gift" or the filmstrip: "Seek the Lord First"; (3) short talks by general chairman and cultivation chairman; (4) booklets: "Seek the Lord First," "Prove Your Love," or "Why Does God Give Men Money?"; (5) two layman's talks of about 3 minutes each; (6) discussion; (7) making of pledges (or these may also be picked up by the visitors on the next Sunday in the homes); (8) Closing remarks and devotion by the pastor.

Leaders should feel responsible to call on those who have not been reached by any specific EMSV or program or on those who have not committed themselves. Callers for call-backs should be chosen with utmost care — usually not the same visitor as on the first visit. These visitors should be especially spiritual-minded, tactful, courteous, good listeners; they should know the story well.

There should be as much concern shown for the last and the least as for the first and the foremost. The problem is that often most time is spent with those who need it least, and the least time is spent with those who need it most.

The EMSV Is a Good Method of Ministry

A Michigan layman was asked by his congregation to direct the Every Member Stewardship Visit (for Christian giving) without having had previous experience as a director. Before going to EMSV manuals and other helps, he went to the Bible to discover what the task might be. He started by asking himself basic questions as to the nature of the task and studied the Scriptures to learn what God's plan might be. He succeeded in outlining a program that followed the fundamental principles he discovered in the

Bible. He developed the following stewardship objectives for EMSV's (for teaching the grace of giving), which he has been conducting in other places ever since. He says:

"Two sets of questions are first answered to gain Scriptural objectives in the program. They are:

1. What shall be the content of a program that will contain and cause to be accomplished that which is God-pleasing in every respect, that will give all glory to God? What would be in conformity with His Word and will? What would communicate Scriptural motivation to all members of the parish?

2. How can the people's hearts be won? How can we seek to get them to do what should be accomplished for the Kingdom's sake? How can we get them to assume positions of leadership? How can we overcome the natural resistance which is always evident? How can such a program be made lively, interesting, educational, inspirational, informative, challenging?

"In accomplishing approach number 1, the program itself must be built effectively around God's Word, using it as a basis and setting forth the wonderful truths of Scripture to be used in reaching people in such ways as:

A. Group meetings at church or family circle meetings, led by laymen who have been instructed and who in the course of their instruction become more convinced themselves, believe as never before, and act and perform as never before.

B. Train leaders and workers or visitors (canvassers) in the basic Scriptural principles of stewardship and giving, with a strong emphasis on practical application. Not only is it necessary to emphasize God's great gifts to us but also just what an adequate or a reasonable expression of OUR LOVE to HIM is in terms of the grace of proportionate giving. How can a man say with his tongue that he loves his Savior, and then continue in bad habits of giving Him the leftovers? Such bad practices need to be changed, and sometimes it takes rather plain talk on the part of other believers to help get such habits changed.

C. *Educate* and inspire the whole congregation in a *well-planned* program.

"In accomplishing approach Number 2 — winning the hearts of the people for the program — consider the following: A well-prepared and equipped leader must direct the program and —

A. Speak in such down-to-earth terms that the people will understand and that they will want to listen to him.

B. Have an approach which is personable, humorous in a natural way, and interesting. He must work with them 'standing on common ground' in every way possible."

It is significant to note the questions this leader raised before he started his efforts. Little wonder that he discovered a message of giving that flows from the Gospels and Epistles, and that his method was adopted only to convey adequately what people need to know about giving. It certainly indicates the possibility that many programs are overorganized and that too large a stress can be placed on secondary factors at the expense of primary ones, on method at the expense of the message.

Commitments and Pledges in Relation to the Call

The human side to stewardship and the EMSV is dramatic. God calls through us to challenge for response. The Holy Spirit works within us, awakens us to newness of life, and gives us the impulse to say "Yes" to the call.

But what type of response is to be expected in Christian giving? We believe that the commitment should be made on the basis of percentage giving. Considering sanctification, this seems the best way. God's priest gives as He has blessed. As God gives, man responds in love by giving his predetermined portion — the measure of his love. Many people have objected to pledging a set sum, even in the knowledge that this was not a legal pledge and could be changed if circumstances changed. The fact is that psychologically and spiritually a strong emphasis on pledging a specific sum drives people inward and causes them to reflect pessimistically. The result is that they will pledge the minimum, not the maximum. They think this way: If we earn more, then we will give more. However, this very seldom happens, and good intentions are forgotten. The way to get the most honest commitment is to ask for percentage pledges: a certain percentage of the income, regardless of how high or low it will be in the next year. Some Christians have called this "God's common-sense way of giving," for if income is high, then the gifts will be high, and if the income is average, the gifts will be average, and if income is low, the gift will be low — all in proportion as God has given.

Some may wonder how the church can plan an accurate budget or spending guide if there is to be no pledge of a specific amount. It is a matter of emphasis. We might indicate what amount might be expected as offerings in view of our percentage agreed on. The emphasis in the pledge should be on the firstfruits and on the percentage, while the amount results from these two factors.

A suggested pledge card that incorporates the concept of proportionate giving is the following: "My Pledge to My Savior — As my response to God's great love in the forgiveness of my sins through Christ and as a faithful steward of God's spiritual and material gifts, I plan with God's help to give of my time and talents in the sharing of the Gospel as opportunities present themselves, and to set aside _____% of my income as firstfruits for God's local and worldwide work through my church. *According to my expected income,* I plan to give: $_____ WEEKLY for the local and worldwide work of our Savior.

(Signed) _____."

What about the collection and fulfillment of pledges? Response is gained on the level that the message is given; if pledges are obtained under pressure, they must be collected under pressure; if pledges are received after careful education in the facts of firstfruit, percentage giving by God's grace, a change of giving habits can be expected and the offerings will be given by normal processes of motivation through regular teaching and preaching.

The principle of "No education without commitment" is important because people tend to talk and dream about what they want to do, but it is difficult for them to put the idea into action. Jesus showed grave concern toward uncommitted persons. When an effective training program or EMSV is completed, the member should take a new step of faith in the form of an enlarged commitment. The effort to get a commitment shows a concern for the person's spiritual welfare, for he cannot long deny Scriptural knowledge of stewardship without soon denying his faith. Man's sinful nature remains "untied" if the "saint-side" does not declare its intention by the power of the Spirit. We owe it to ourselves to plan our service and offerings and to express our faith in a pledge to the God of Promise.

Use of Envelopes and Offerings as Forms for Gospel Response

It seems wise to use envelopes in our day, for this assures an accurate accounting to the government for tax purposes, and it helps the individual keep an accurate record. But what is the best system of envelopes: unit, duplex, triplex, or multiple envelopes for many causes?

There is something disconcerting to people who have been motivated to give a generous percentage of their income weekly when they are faced with all types of extra envelopes, and the envelopes then are divided into many causes. Some believe that the more envelopes people are given, the more they will give. Such a method does something to Biblical theology, and it's no good. See the fragmentized giving that many Christians are asked to do under plans that offer a multitude of envelopes.

Much is lost when people are constantly faced and bombarded with the necessity to hand out a few dollars here and there to persistent church promotors. Something is wrong when basic church needs are turned into causes that are segmented, and then gifts are urged through great promotional campaigns. There are grossly detrimental effects when the individual faces many appeals for local needs, such as current, missions, building, chimes, charities, pet projects, and other specials together with a multiplicity of mission and welfare collections from the church body.

Various campaigns and special drives are poor substitutes for Christian stewardship and giving. They seem to be an admission that stewardship education and training in giving has failed and now promotion is the answer. The more frequently campaigns and extra envelopes are resorted to, the less effective they usually become. Special campaigns and more offering envelopes are false remedies that apply only to the symptoms of the illness, while good educational programs would get at the illness itself, the source of the problem.

We believe that there are great advantages in using the unified plan with unit envelopes. This makes easier the operation of a system of accounting and auditing and offers a better financial arrangement. People are no longer approached for various "causes" that are essentially *the* cause. The unified plan effectively faces the problem of arbitrarily dividing motivation and the act of giving into various categories. There is just one pledge for the entire work.

The unified approach more easily allows for proper motive of giving for *the* cause. In multiple offering systems there is a temptation toward feverish promotion with the advantage going to the best promoters. The unified approach requires consultation and widens the participation of the planning in

153

sharing the offerings equitably. It presents a clear picture of the church's total program in one interrelated mission. If this is not done, people become confused by all the appeals. It helps to dispel the impression that the church is primarily concerned with money.

The unified plan must avoid cutting short world missions through a lack of year-round mission education efforts and sufficient discussion when the world mission budget is set. People must be given an opportunity for self-expression in voluntary special offerings for world missions and charities without dividing it for local purposes, or otherwise their individual rights have been taken away. This means that members be given the opportunity to direct offerings for certain causes, if they choose.

The Call to Plan for Corporate Stewardship of Funds

The unified approach calls for careful corporate stewardship. Someone has defined corporate stewardship as "the orderly practice of mobilizing the total dedicated potential of the whole church, based on the conviction that this is a trust from God and fully implementing His will in the building of His kingdom at home and in all the world." Financially, corporate stewardship is the proper and wise use of all offerings brought by all members for the Lord's work. This stewardship is exercised when the membership adopts a budget or spending guide. It is also exercised when all members are good managers of their total income. Christians need to learn that their personal and church stewardship actions are corporate because in Christ they are "corporate."

Corporate stewardship begins with mutual concern between one another that God's gifts to all the members are properly used and properly distributed in their personal lives, a generous share being given to Him through the church. Members have a stewardship or ministry to each other to encourage and exhort to generous giving. Members also should be concerned that other members are not withholding a portion from God. Then the congregation is ready to practice corporate stewardship in the division of the offerings. Corporate stewardship requires a proper and wise use of funds in the congregation's local work. Too much emphasis on "creature comforts" and pet projects must be avoided. The division of offerings between local and world responsibilities should be decided by sensitive consciences. In the face of a world mission crisis, congregations should avoid unnecessary expenditures in their facilities at the cost of world missions.

The matter of establishing priorities for budget items cannot be overemphasized. After this is done the congregation should not adopt special projects that have not been adopted in the budget so that more important priorities will not be sidetracked. It would be unwise to resolve on air conditioning or a tower in the middle of the year when no funds have been budgeted for them. Equipment and other capital investments should be planned, and then the plan should be followed according to established priorities.

Concerning the receiving of offerings in the worship services, this should be done with a lack of promotion but in the most worshipful atmosphere. This is no time to exhort and harangue people to bring more money to the Lord. This is no time for jokes about people "pinning their gifts" or about a "silent collection."

Regarding offerings in the Sunday school, it should be considered that if the educational and worship services on Sunday are a unit and if giving is an act of worship, then offerings should be brought in one act. If education is a part of the church's function, then general treasury offerings ought to cover the education in Sunday school. We believe that children should have envelopes and that they too should bring their offerings in the worship service itself.

Concerning dues and offerings in organizations (for example, youth and women's groups), some congregations which are following a grace system and encouraging proportionate giving do not have any offerings in organizations. Instead the members do all their giving to the church treasury, and from the church treasury the organization is allowed a certain amount of money to do its work. This is a great encouragement for youth to adopt good giving habits and to give in worship. It should be noted that all offerings need not be placed into envelopes and that various charities, public and private, are also worthy of thoughtful assistance.

None of this rules out special offerings. What it says is that the general plan and approach, if it is to be expressive of the grace of giving, should be a unified approach. If any group sees an absolute need and feels it is justified, then it will undoubtedly wish to resolve on a special offering, but only within the concept of proportionate giving. Even in special offerings people should be reminded of the basic giving habits of the dedicated Christian, otherwise more damage can be done than what the financial gains are worth. However, when congregations undertake a true educational program with a strong emphasis on firstfruit or generous percentage giving, they will discover that generally their basic needs are covered, including future expansion programs, since they will be budgeted beforehand — and whatever debts accrue from building programs may be paid through regular offerings.

Terminology as Form of Communication

"Words people use are a map of the world in which they live," declared a professor of sociology. There are certain words leaders may use which indicate that their vision is limited, and there are words which show that they live in a world with broad horizons. You can find both kinds of words used in stewardship terminology. Words are useful only to the extent that they convey meaning. An attempt should be made to select the best possible words to convey the best stewardship concepts.

We would suggest an interchange of the words: "the

management of life" and "the stewardship of life." The overuse of a word such as stewardship in congregational activities tends to deaden its effect. We believe the word "management" offers an excellent synonym for variety's sake. One of the meanings of this word is "the skillful use of means to accomplish a purpose" (Funk and Wagnalls). To manage means to handle, to control, to treat with care. Managing one's life and possessions to the glory of God and for the good of others is stewardship.

Several favorite stewardship words of the past ought to be replaced with new words more descriptive of what the concept and aspirations actually are. The word "dues" has been dropped because it conveyed an entirely wrong meaning for a church offering. Several phrases that need restudy are: "Over the Top" and "Fair Share." "OVER THE TOP" is often the report to the congregation or area churches after a modest budget is reached. Over the top of what? Over the top of the *bottom?* If a budget has a minimum goal, dare the church talk about going over the top? When the budget is shaved, pared, and cut to the immediate, bare essentials in order to place it in line with expected receipts (not according to actual needs), can this be called the "top"? Admittedly such a figure is the bottom. Then it should be called just that — "Over the *bottom.*" Such a reference will keep everyone more conscious of unmet responsibilities. It makes a world of difference in people's thinking!

Then there's the "fair share." Some mistakenly spell it a "fare share," possibly symbolic of the concept some people have of their world mission duties — a *fare* share, as though members were paying a fare somewhere! Some see a fair share as being the equation of "members x $25 (or whatever the average is) equals a fair share." What's "fair" about it? The only fair approach to the church's mission is to teach all members porportionate giving that leads to growing efforts for outreach. Members of the same family use such phrases as "Do your share" and "Do your part." God does not dole out shares for His work, but He gives each one talents he is to use according to the measure of the gift.

More care ought to be used also in using the words "realistic" or "attainable." A realistic program? Realistic in relation to what? When Scriptural realities are left out in the church's setting of plans, they cannot be classified as realistic. There is no Scriptural realism that leaves Christ out of the picture. Attainable? By what measure? By past standards of leadership and education? By new insights into a program of giving and mission education? By the power of the Spirit? It all depends upon who says it and from what background and from what plans for action, does it not?

The word "sacrifice" ought to be used much more carefully in stewardship language, we believe. What is a sacrifice? How can it be measured? If most Christians would give 11 percent of their income for spiritual causes, how many would be sacrificing? and on what basis? People who do not sacrifice do not know what the word means. People who sacrifice usually do not talk about it and do not realize they are doing it. Sacrifice appears to be a word which should receive considerable study, for it is an act little understood in America. It would be well to find other ways to describe the totality of response included in sacrifice.

People do not get a proper picture of the nature of stewardship through directed programs no matter how good they are when they are called "campaigns" or "drives." Someone has said facetiously: "Campaign has a 'pain' in it. And who wants to be driven in a 'drive'?" It is highly doubtful whether these two words can avoid conveying a negative picture of stewardship efforts. We suggest that they be dropped altogether, for other words present more accurately the true intent of stewardship efforts.

Stewardship Ministry and Professional Fund Raisers

It seems odd that many congregations would admit that they have failed in their financial stewardship in such a basic way that they have needed outside help, but they have admitted it, and they have employed professional fund raisers. Without a question some of this has been a tremendous blessing and very wholesome. As a general venture it is possible that this assistance has awakened some congregations to some of their inherent weaknesses and alerted them to take some excellent steps. However, money and the lack of it was the motivation to employ professionals (even from outside the denomination).

Byfield and Shaw make these observations: "The real question about the fund-raising concerns lies, not in their methods but in the fact that they exist. For basically their task involves the use of various techniques to enable Christian people to fulfill one aspect of their Christian vocation! Suppose, for example, a church should engage a firm to help increase its Sunday attendance through the use of promotional devices, special meetings, and so on? While the church may well undertake such a project for itself, the hiring of a public relations firm to do it would cause raised eyebrows, to say the least. To carry the comparison to its ridiculous conclusion, what would we say of a church that hired a firm of specialists to help combat immorality within the congregation? And yet morality, church attendance, and Christian stewardship have this in common: They are all simply aspects of the total Christian life. There are real questions involved in the employment of outsiders to accomplish any of them!" [9]

Since theology is the basis for the stewardship program, we believe it is imperative that the professionals, when used, should be from *within* the denomination and that they should make certain that the methods serve the message and theology of the church. If they are really needed, which we are not prepared to accept fully, professionals should be asked to do what the congregation feels incapable of doing because the membership as a whole will follow the leadership of local leaders too listlessly. Thus professionals can best fill the role of diagnosticians as "brothers" of the group.

Christ's teachings about giving show that at no time does He suggest money-raising schemes as means of financing His church through the covenant plan. He makes it clear, too, that His house is not a house of merchandise.

Do such money-raising methods as suppers, sales, and bazaars really help the work of the church? At what price is the financial assistance bought? Is the time given worth it? Should the church act as a merchant? Why not give the clothes outright to the needy? Why not use the time instead for evangelism calls and for personal mission work? What about the offense to merchants and others in the community? Is the adoption of these methods an admission that the church has not taught the grace of giving, or has done it ineffectively?

Is a Christian really giving when he patronizes church sales and suppers, when he has only received his money's worth as he would have in any good store or restaurant? At times donations are received which would have been refused or not freely given as an outright offering. Money-raising schemes stir up a motivation for giving and serving which can exist without the power of Christian faith and the grace of God. Every plan which puts people "on the spot," or which appeals to pride, is improper in God's kingdom.

Moneymaking schemes are often a distinct hindrance to the development of the spirit of Christian giving and the spiritual goals of the church. Where the dollars must be coaxed from people by commercial plans, there the spirit of worldliness is bound to prevail. It is necessary to "raise" money only when Christians fail to give it.

In most cases such affairs are unprofitable both in the number of hours spent and the amount of money earned per worker's hour. People donate the materials, do the work, and then pay a price for the things they buy, some of which they at times do not really want. Time is too valuable for that kind of activity; it would be more profitably spent in service and witnessing tasks. We do not mean to disparage church affairs such as suppers for fellowship. Congregations will do well to sponsor fellowship meetings. However, in these as in any other church affairs financial profit should be incidental, not intentional.

Some feel that bazaars, sales, and suppers (for profit) foster Christian fellowship. They do have some fellowship value. Experience has shown, however, that this fellowship usually involves the same few people who are the faithful workers every time the call is given. Too often the fellowship values claimed do not obtain — at least there is no *Christian* fellowship where edifying was experienced. On the contrary, feelings have sometimes been hurt through competition between members, and some have done less than others. This problem shows up much more in these affairs than in group work in the regular service and evangelism program of the church.

By its very nature the church depends upon gifts and offerings since it has no physical commodity to sell. "Give!" was the Savior's will, not "Buy and Sell." The church has no reason to enter into competitive buying and selling for the purpose of maintaining its work. People should look to the church for salvation — not for sales.

The change away from indirect giving methods should be done through counseling in the spiritual aspects involved. These money-raising schemes may be overcome and supplanted by a grace of generous Christian giving through the teaching of proportionate giving. A positive program of Christian service in keeping with the purposes of the church should be substituted for these various schemes.

(Related indirectly to commercialism, we feel, is the payment of perquisites to clergymen for ministerial acts. This payment for pastoral services has been swiftly passing from the scene, but it is a bit surprising that it still is much in evidence. Taking money at the time of baptisms, weddings, funerals, or any other official ministry to people's specific needs finds the pastor in the awkward position of seeming to accept payment for individual services for which he receives a salary. Most clergymen today agree that it is unwise to accept such fees or perquisites for administering the sacraments, dispensing the Gospel, or any official act. Rather, congregations should be urged to pay adequate salaries, and all offers of perquisites be turned over to the church as an offering for the occasion.)

[1] Eduard Schweizer, *Church Order in the New Testament* (London: SCM Press, 1959), pp. 14, 15; distributed in the U.S.A. by Alec R. Allenson, Inc., of Naperville, Ill.

[2] The Layman's Movement, *Living My Religion on My Job* (New York: Wainright House, 1962), pp. 19, 20.

[3] Philadelphia: Westminster Press, 1962, pp. 16, 63.

[4] Robert E. Coleman, *The Master Plan of Evangelism* (Westwood, N. J.: Fleming H. Revell Co., 1963), pp. 21, 78.

[5] Paul Lindemann, *Christian Stewardship and Its Modern Implications* (St. Louis: Concordia Publishing House, 1933), pp. 32-38.

[6] Brian Rice, *What Is Christian Giving?* (London: SCM Press, 1959), pp. 9, 25, 26.

[7] Rice, p. 14.

[8] The author's stewardship book for teen-agers, *Live!* is useful both for discussion groups and for individual reading among youth. St. Louis: Church-Craft Pictures, 1965.

[9] Richard Byfield and James P. Shaw, *Your Money and Your Church* (Garden City, N. Y.: Doubleday & Co., Inc., 1959).

Chapter 8

Stewardship Tools for the Group Ministry

The stewardship teaching efforts suggest the use of visual and printed aids whose scope and subject matter will adequately cover the Biblical stewardship concept and the objectives outlined. Often these stewardship tools tell only a little about the church budget and present only a few activities of the church and then ask for a pledge of financial support. Too many are long on exhortation and short on sound education in Christian giving in matters where people are uninformed. These tools should grow creatively out of the theology of stewardship and be used in a concrete way to meet the spiritual and educational needs of the members. Stewardship tools offer an opportunity to challenge the spirituality of all members and direct them to a higher level of faith.

Flipcharts

The flipchart ought not be a short 5- or 10-minute presentation of exhortatory material, but a 15- to 25-minute educational treatment of Christian stewardship or giving. Salesmen do not sell cars or TV sets in 5 or 10 minutes, and let us not expect to "sell" people on changing their stewardship attitudes or giving habits in such a short time. If the message is relevant, members will be interested in a longer presentation. Why should people resent a longer visit? Adequate time is needed to teach effectively.

It seems that too many flipcharts still miss the proper objectives of stewardship and are little more than promotion couched in the seller's terms, "If you do what we suggest, the church will benefit." Messages often tell about the congregation's work and then ask people to give proportionately to do the work. Instead the message should be presented in the members' terms and talk about "how the individual grows in grace through grateful and responsible use of money to the glory of God." Flipcharts ought to help people look into their attitudes and motives rather than look at the church's demands upon their income.

Stewardship departments of denominational headquarters offer flipcharts to be studied for possible use. There are other flipcharts or booklets available through interdenominational agencies, messages that incorporate the objectives and philosophy studied in this book. The following are such materials.

"Seek the Lord First" is a 16-page booklet that is designed for use in the EMSV, and it presents a concise summary of Christian giving on the basis of Matt. 6:33. Each page has appropriate art work and a message encouraging firstfruit (generous percentage) giving coming from Christ's encouragement to seek first the kingdom of God.[1]

"Prove Your Love" is a 16-page booklet (color) based on Paul's exhortation to the Corinthian Christians in 2 Cor. 8:8. "Prove the sincerity of your love." Its message shows how God poured His love into the lives of all Christians, how He feeds and strengthens this love, and how Christians are to express their love in a life of witnessing, service, and giving. It particularly stresses the importance of proportionate giving.[2]

"God's Helping Hands" is a 12-page booklet (full color) for the EMSV telling how God made the Christian's hands instruments through which He works and through which we care for ourselves and for others in the world. It tells how the Father's hands made and govern us, how the Son's hands saved us, and how our hands are guided by the Spirit's power. It shows our hands lifted in praise, opened in loving service, and reaching out to invite others. It tells how helping hands do Christ's work and how giving hands send the Gospel to the ends of the earth. The topic source is Annie

Johnston Flint's poem "Christ Has No Hands but Our Hands." [3]

"You and Your Pulpit" — 16-page booklet which features 14 full-color illustrations with messages on the Christian vocation and calling according to 1 Peter 2:9; it is suitable for the EMSV and group meetings at the church. The booklet brings a pointed message on the priesthood of all believers and shows each believer's life as a "pulpit" to convey the Gospel to others. It provides practical applications for the life of every Christian. [4]

"Why Does God Give Men Money?" — a 16-page booklet which provides a summary message from Scripture about the Christian philosophy and the meaning of money in the life of a Christian. It encourages careful expenditures and giving habits which match the Christian faith. [5]

"The Step Forward" — a 20 page booklet which supplies a clear commentary on the Christian struggle between the new man and the old man. It provides lively statements to portray struggle in taking a step forward in worship, Communion, Bible study, use of time and talents, commitment of time and talents, understanding and using possessions and money, and determining the size of offerings. [6]

"The Story of Our Offering Envelopes" — a 16-page booklet that tells the story of offerings and the use of church envelopes. It tells of the greatest offering of all — how God poured His love upon mankind and upon His church. It tells how the church and its members now become a blessing to the world. Telling of hindrances to generous giving, the message proclaims Christian principles for giving. [7]

Visual Aids

The Gift — an outstanding motion picture that gives a quick review of our Savior's life and its meaning to all Christians. After showing what sin has done to us and our world and how God's act of love came to our rescue, it demonstrates that the whole man is involved in the whole mission of God's kingdom. Through the medium of animated and meaningful color art and pictures it strives to leave a lasting impression of the stewardship of life. This film provides a tremendous message and motivation for stewardship. Produced by the National Council of Churches, it is available from denominational visual aid centers.

Seek the Lord First — a color filmstrip presenting the New Testament principle of firstfruit, generous, proportionate giving based on the Savior's exhortation in Matt. 6:33. In 44 frames it shows how Christians are to express their faith in giving God priority in their lives. The filmstrip package includes a recording, leader's guide, and a pocket-size flip-chart.[8]

Test of Faith — an excellent filmstrip (black and white) that presents a dramatic portrayal of the blessings of proportionate giving, pointing out that it is a test of faith. The case for proportionate giving is stated very well. It concludes with 25 discussion frames on the subject.[9]

The Plan — an excellent stewardship filmstrip (color, 64 frames, 11 minutes) for teen-agers, based upon God's plan in Christ for all people. It provides the necessary foundation for stewardship and speaks clearly to youth. An excellent guide is supplied.[10]

Me in a Pulpit? — This filmstrip package is designed to help teach the New Testament concept of the priesthood of all believers. It should help Christians understand better their Christian calling and vocation and to stimulate them toward a total commitment to their high calling in Jesus Christ. The filmstrip kit contains one 54-frame color filmstrip with recording, two copies of the leader's guide, a copy of the 16-page booklet "You and Your Pulpit" designed for the EMSV, and a 72-page paperback book "Your Pulpit in Life" (available separately) that is a complete text on the Christian vocation and calling for the laity.[11]

That's Where the Money Goes! and *Planning Where the Money Goes* — color filmstrips with recordings in two parts that incorporate a Christian philosophy of money and a practical budget accounting for the Christian family. Filled with practical ideas, it alerts people to Christ's love which is the key to the use of money. The filmstrip package also includes the book *Where Does Your Money Go?* (available separately) together with a flipchart "Why Does God Give Men Money?" for use in the EMSV and a "Christian Family Account Book." [12]

Stewardship — Why Do We Live? (F-331), *Guide for Living* (F-332), *Guide for Serving* (F-333), *Guide for Giving* (F-334). This series of filmstrips with study guides is exceptionally good material for a study course to be used in organizations, Bible classes, or for a series of stewardship meetings. [13]

General Educational Tools and Media

Stewardship tools should be utilized in a process of nurturing, growing, and becoming. This means that the educational tools used in the EMSV are only a part of the total stewardship program. Stewardship is so basic to the whole church life that the use of stewardship tools must not be relegated to a few weeks or just one month of each year. Stewardship is more than an agency activity or a programed thrust for November. Many congregations tend to expect 6-week educational program to do something which is lacking during the other 46 weeks. People should be helped when they need help — year round — and the church's ministry should be keyed to that fact.

If a congregation expects to have an effective stewardship program that strives to meet Scriptural goals, it will be necessary to have a stewardship committee which has studied and outlined a well-defined plan and selected tools to do the job. The committee should ask itself: What should we teach God's people about the general stewardship of life, Christian giving, and mission education? When this question has been fully answered, then the committee will see that there are three major areas into which the committee should divide itself. Each subcommittee should study *materials* within its area of concern and make reports and recommendations on these tools to the entire committee. Stewardship committees have too often worked with the broad concerns of stewardship without delegating any one specific concern to subcommittees with the result that "everybody's business has been nobody's business." This lack of delegation has resulted in a general confusion where the chairman has found it impossible to read, digest, and share with the committee all the materials that come into his hands. Through subcommittees the chairman delegates these responsibilities and asks for specific reports and recommendations at each meeting.

A good stewardship committee will encourage the pastor to preach straightforward, grace-centered sermons on various stewardship topics at regular intervals, not just in November. Also, the pastor should plan a thorough, heart-to-heart talk with all of his church officers where there is concentrated discussion on the subject of firstfruit, generous percentage giving. No officer should be allowed to be free from real heart-searching in this matter, and it can best be handled at a time other than October or November.

All Sunday school teachers should be good examples of the stewardship message and be aware of the many opportunities to bring students to a point of greater commitment. A lesson on stewardship and giving is not taught well if the teachers do not set an example by their commitment to the truths they teach. Effective teaching does not take place if teachers are ignoring the suggestions for action that are learned on the basis of the Word. Adults in Sunday school ought to study and discuss such good stewardship Bible studies as R. C. Rein's *First Fruits*[14] and *Adventures in Christian Stewardship;*[15] Raymond Olson's *Stewards Appointed;*[16] and Paul G. Bretscher's *Life Under Grace.*[17]

The stewardship committee should provide a good supply of stimulating stewardship tracts and folders. They ought to be given to people occasionally on personal calls or at a church service. Some tracts (among a large selection) available for interdenominational use from the American Lutheran Publicity Bureau (2112 Broadway, New York 23, N.Y.) are the following: "When $10 − $1 = $10"; "A Man Has to Live, Doesn't He?"; "I Was An Embezzler"; "You Are a Christian Farmer"; "It's in Your Hands"; and "Guests of God."

New converts and new members are to be approached at the time they join the church to understand the grace-centered message which the congregation follows in stewardship and Christian giving. Possibly they can be led in a discussion of some stewardship booklet as "Prove Your Love" (ALPB), "Seek the Lord First" (Church-Craft), or "Why Does God Give Men Money?" (Church-Craft)

Charlie W. Shedd suggests a year-round educational program in his stimulating book *How to Develop a Tithing Church*. He shows how constant education gives the congregation a real impact through the commitment of its members. His congregation presses for generous proportionate giving, as he states: "We are not concerned with your share of our budget! What matters is your share of God's income." [18] Shedd says that theirs is a "study the Scripture and see what Christ says to you," and "start somewhere and develop as the Lord leads" plan.[19] From them the teaching of stewardship and giving has long arms and steady hands. The leaders of his congregation write to the members: "We want you to clearly understand that we do not think you can be what you should be as a member of our church until you have settled the stewardship between you and Christ who gave His all for you! We urge you to keep an open mind and to develop a prayerful heart towards His teachings. We say it again, 'We do not believe that you can be that kind of member which Christ needs in this church unless you remain open to divine direction.' "[20]

How to Raise Men and Money in the Church[21] is a book which tells how to conduct the EMSV and to use

170

proper tools according to the concept expounded in these pages. The book gives directions for organization of a training program in a simple way.

Notes for Chapter 8

[1] Church-Craft Pictures, Inc., 4222 Utah, St. Louis, Mo. 63116

[2] American Lutheran Publicity Bureau, 2112 Broadway, New York 23, N. Y.

[3] New York: American Lutheran Publicity Bureau.

[4] St. Louis: Church-Craft Pictures.

[5] St. Louis: Church-Craft Pictures.

[6] Iowa District West, 1317 Tower Drive, Fort Dodge, Iowa.

[7] New York: American Lutheran Publicity Bureau.

[8] Stewardship FA-19. St. Louis: Church-Craft Pictures.

[9] Produced by the American Lutheran Church, 426 S. Fifth St., Minneapolis 15, Minn.

[10] *The Plan.* Reformed Church in America, Stewardship Council, 475 Riverside Dr., New York 27, N. Y.

[11] Stewardship FA-25. St. Louis: Church-Craft Pictures.

[12] Stewardship Kit FA-26. St. Louis: Church-Craft Pictures.

[13] Stewardship, Vol. V, by John E. Herrmann. St. Louis: Church-Craft Pictures.

[14] St. Louis: Concordia Publishing House, 1959.

[15] St. Louis: Concordia Publishing House, 1955.

[16] Minneapolis: Augsburg Publishing House, 1958.

[17] St. Louis: Concordia Publishing House, 1961. Adult Bible Discussion Guide in 13 parts.

[18] Charlie W. Shedd, *How to Develop a Tithing Church* (Nashville: Abingdon Press, 1961), p. 19.

[19] Shedd, p. 41.

[20] Shedd, p. 116.

[21] New York: American Lutheran Publicity Bureau, 1956.

Chapter 9

The Stewardship Horizon: Unlimited Possibilities

We are called as disciples to be on God's mission with all the resources God gives. Yet the whole world is being influenced and "evangelized" by many conflicting philosophies of men but not with the Gospel of Jesus Christ. Partial commitment by Christians as a result of partial Gospel challenges will not solve the dilemma. The church's long-haul task of world evangelism requires a continuing program of education in the Word — anything less is a dubious stop-gap approach and will not get the long-haul job done. This task, we must remember, is inherent in the covenant of the Gospel.

May we expect greatly enlarged stewardship activities by the power of the Holy Spirit? The 19th General Council of the World Alliance of Reformed Churches in its August 1964 meeting in Germany asked some searching questions: "(1) What evidence of the Spirit's work of renewal do you see in your congregation? (2) What difference do you expect the Spirit's coming to make in the life work and witness of your congregation? (3) What room is allowed in your personal life and in your congregation for the work of the Spirit? (4) What do you regard as the chief obstacles in the way of the renewing work of the Spirit in the church and in the life of Christians today? (5) How can the pastoral ministry be renewed by the Creator Spirit? (6) What steps can be taken to renew the work and witness of church members? (7) In what new direction is the Spirit calling the church today?" These questions are worthy of consideration by every leadership group.

The World Mission Scope of the Plan

The scope of our Savior's mission is universal. Take away the feature that "He died for *all,*" and its whole character is altered. He is no mere "American" or "tribal" Savior. The Son of God lived and loved, died and rose again for nothing less than the *entire* world. The bare truth of sin in the world and the Savior from sin requires its universality and calls for conveying the Good News to the whole world of sinners.

"Ye shall be witnesses . . . BOTH in Jerusalem AND in Judea AND in Samaria AND unto the uttermost part of the earth" (Acts 1:8). "Both . . . and!" The witness is to be local and worldwide. The doors of churches should be wide enough to receive all who need love, fellowship, and spirital care, and they should lead out to the nation and the world.

God makes no distinction between home missions and foreign missions in the Gospels. They are but two different phases of the same task. Local and worldwide missions are *one* mission. The distinction between home and foreign missions is only a practical one. There is not so much work to be done locally that world responsibilities dare be denied. A congregation exists for the world; it has no choice of "either . . . or." God allows only a "both . . . and" vision; His Gospel is universal, for Christ died for the local people and for those 10,000 miles away.

Sometime ago we spoke at a mission rally held in the National Guard Armory of a midwest city. On a large banner on the wall was placed the motto of the 138th Infantry Regiment: "Even Hell Cannot Stop Us!" It haunted us every moment while singing, praying, and preaching, not so much for its supernatural claim, but the thought that came to mind of the promise of God for His church: "I will build my church; and the gates of hell shall not prevail against it." In the face of the motto of the 138th Regiment and its war record, the "war record" of Christian soldiers marched before our eyes: some very good indeed; others, very poor — excuses, inactivity, demands to be coddled, side-stepping responsibilities, some giving grave offense against the Savior, and others showing indications of lack of heart. Satan spends his energies on grasping power and robbing the Savior of the fruits of His Calvary victory. To ignore Satan is to be enveloped in deception and spiritual complacency. To magnify his power is to be guilty of folly. To fear him is to be faithless. If the church is to meet the challenge of this day, she must gird for the battle in which "the gates of hell shall not prevail."

The war is on! One of the most severe struggles the world has seen is raging. It's not a shooting war, but it is deadly serious. It's a *spiritual* war against the secret powers of Satan! In this war we must win, or lose all! The church is the battlefield, and it must plot the strategy for an all-out offensive. The ammunition is *words,* and they should convey the Word of Truth.

Even while many congregations have been making commendable advances, the church generally has been letting sectarian agencies preempt its position — and it has made excuses. God opened the doors for entrance *now.* Present opportunity cannot be stored up for future use — when that is attempted, it is lost. The church will look mighty silly 5 or 10 years from now with money on hand, *if these same doors are then closed.* Prayers dare not be: "Lord keep the doors open until we can get ready to enter," but must be: "Lord, make us ready now for the doors that are opened by Thee for entrance today."

Seldom has the church faced as many open doors as today. This is one of the few times in history when resources are so abundant that impressive statistics of growth are possible by efforts and giving standards which merely skim the cream of our resources. There should be a consciousness of using resources more responsibly in a civilization that is lost in its hell-bound effort to reach the ultimate in scientific achievement and in ease of living. Sometimes vision hardly goes beyond the four walls of the local church. The gulf between resources and performance cannot be bridged by doubts, by excuses, or by pointing to the fact that some progress is being made.

When is Christianity at its truest and best? Surely not in its pride of property, nor in its elegance of ritual, nor in its glory in numbers. These things take the eye and capture the imagination, but what else can they do? The true might of the church is not in its visible resources but in the heart of each individual.

A Strategy for Our Day

Today's strategy involves the principle that the church is responsible for all those for whom Jesus assumed responsibility. The church is also to accept the costly liability which results from identification with the task which Jesus assumed at the price of His death.

John Bright suggests: "We are to stop trifling with our historic task. . . . We must each of us rise to our calling; we must become a missionary people. . . . We came, then, to the New Testament asking for a program of action by which we might further the victory of Christ, and we have received our answer: I give you no program, but a calling — to be *the church!*" [1]

Today's strategy involves the principle that today's open doors be entered *today*. "Go ye also into the vineyard!" (Matt. 20:4) seems to be as current as the first day it was spoken. It says: "Don't stand idle in the market place! Don't leave your money uninvested or use it unwisely! Invest your time and money in God's kingdom!" What farmer today would allow his hired help to spend only three hours per day in the harvest fields when the grain is ripe and the harvest is in danger of being lost? How can church members, called into the vineyard by their Lord, be allowed to give leftover hours and leftover money (very many less than 3 percent) to gain the harvest of souls that is *now* passing into eternal perdition?

A strategy for our day might be gained in part from a

mission compact signed by Missionaries Carey, Marshman, and Ward of India on Oct. 7, 1805. In part it read: "It is absolutely necessary: (1) That we set an infinite value upon immortal souls. (2) That we gain all information of the snares and delusions in which these heathen are held. (3) That we abstain from all those things which would increase their prejudices against the Gospel. (4) That we watch all opportunities for good. (5) That we keep to the example of Paul and make the great subject of our preaching Christ the Crucified. (6) That we be constant in prayer to fit us for the discharge of these laborious and unutterably important labors. (7) That we give ourselves unreservedly to this glorious cause. Let us never think that our time, our gifts, our strength, our families, or even the clothes we wear are our own."

Faith Takes Us to the Stewardship Horizons

Saving faith leads to implicit trust. This trust is simply the willingness to take God at His Word even if that Word seems impossible. Faith is a matter of man's letting the Gospel of forgiveness be central in his life and actions. The riches of God's resources are the bank on which this faith depends.

Christians have often made the mistake of overemphasizing the Christian's faith at the expense of the grace of God, which amounts to "having faith in faith." E. J. Friedrich says the results of this are always tragic. He writes: "Faith is then no longer regarded as something that God works in us by His grace and as a free gift from Him, but as an act of man by which he of his own free will and by his own decision renounces evil and cooperates with God in working out his own salvation. According to this erroneous concept, God would only begin our salvation, and we would have to complete it ourselves. . . . It would, in fact, tend to make our faith man-centered instead of Christ-centered. Saving faith, thank God, is not something we must accomplish for ourselves; it is not something we must do to make ourselves worthy of the grace of God. On the contrary, faith comes to us as a gracious benediction from the hand of God." [2]

Stewardship plans of man, no matter how great and ingenious, are frustrating when devoid of trust in the promises of God. The new Israel faces the threshold of the most thrilling, challenging frontier: *the frontier of faith!*

Jesus gave the answer to stewardship problems too, when He said: "According to your *faith* be it unto you!" (Matt. 9:29). Two blind men know Christ can heal. Do they believe that He will heal *them?* "Yes, Lord!" Then Jesus touched their eyes, saying: "According to your *faith* be it unto you!" Their eyes were opened.

The Lord did not say: "According to your *fate* be it unto you." If one is too lazy or faithless to launch out, in expectation of greater things, let him not blame his shallowness on Divine Providence. The fate of the fishermen was that they caught nothing, and now they were asked by Jesus to go out again at a time when conditions were not right. Their answer? It could easily have been: "Now is the wrong time to catch fish." Faith, however, caused them to say: "Nevertheless, Lord, *at Thy word* we will let down the nets." Many church situations could be settled quickly by the response, *"At Thy word,* Lord, we will do it." Many problems of life's management would vanish if a person would react by saying: "It doesn't quite make sense to me, but *at Your word,* Lord, I will put You first and foremost in all my affairs."

The Lord did not say: "According to your *fortune* be it unto you." Humanly speaking it makes a difference if man is struck by bad fortune or not. There are unfavorable conditions with which he must contend. On the other hand, in time of plenty even high income, good crops, and good business in no way assure success. "A man's life consisteth not in the abundance of the things which he possesseth" (Luke 12:15). Prosperity may even drug people into spiritual complacency. Neither good fortune nor its lack will dictate the measure of personal or church success. "It is required in stewards that a man be found *faithful*" (1 Cor. 4:2). Not: You must be found full of wisdom, full of education, full of good health, or found with a full bank account — though all of these may be good. Rather: Be found full of faith!

Often we add up all the human and material resources and then think that this is the last word on the subject. We may figure: so many church members; so many talents; so many dollars we can afford. This is considered the power of the church. And all the time the real strength is being overlooked and ignored. Faith is not a mathematical equation which can predict what can or cannot be done in the church. All the resources are not counted until faith has been included.

Some want to delay tasks because it is not the right time — the time is never right for those who lack faith. It is easier to tackle tasks and try to perform them than to explain why it is felt that they cannot be performed. The greatest failures are failures of faith to go out and act. Many a church meeting would have been changed if someone would have challenged the pessimism expressed and responded to a difficulty with the statement: "*At Thy word*, Lord, we will take action."

Fear paralyzes man into inaction. Unbelief stated in the most acceptable terms runs rampant when man ignores the promises of God. Unbelief restricts God's work, and it gives doubt and fear priority in the place that is rightfully God's.

Concerning our doubts versus the radical realism of the Bible, we are reminded of a cartoon appearing in a London newspaper during the great depression of the 30s in which Will Dysart showed a figure representing God standing with His arm around the shoulder of Jesus. The caption of the picture said: "We are helpless, My Son, the banks have spoken." The church is never at the mercy of IBM projections, the statistical averages, or the *status quo*.

Leaders under the covenant must seek to interpret the issues correctly, respond to the needs intelligently, and do what needs to be done with great spontaneity. The servant of Christ should go out like father Abraham in faith, planning well, but obediently following where God may lead. The walls of the church will not crumble and the institution will not disintegrate as leaders leave their sanctuary and march out in faith. There will no longer be demands to be free of risks, for thereby the child of God is unworthy of faith. The only guarantee the Christian has comes from the promises on which faith is built. The church must lay "tracks" (programs) but none of these can be permanent. The church must ever be ready to pull up "tracks" at any moment and not be too institutionalized in its stewardship form. There must be risk in organization, in method, in success, and in fruit. One thing the church dare not risk: the message. Believers are to risk all on the Word. Of course there is no risk in sowing the Word, for it bears its fruit in due season.

Then prayer is the answer. Faithful prayer has its promise, its price, and its purpose. Its promise is fabulous: see God's guarantees to those who ask in faith. Its price is exacting: in His name we must pray, and this demands an attitude and a conduct worthy of Him. Its purpose is the ultimate adventure of man: to glorify God in prosperity and adversity, in victory and defeat, in life and death — always by His grace.

What great prospects of stewardship adventure lie before those who dare to venture in the Lord's name! Where Christianity has been lethargic and dull, it is because it has chosen to ignore the foundations of faith and refused to accept the sanctions of Christian belief. Stewardship leaders can bring the church face to face with high adventure if they will launch out fearlessly on the basis of what they believe.

Go on to Maturity

As God's chosen instruments believers will bring the full impact of the Gospel upon the spiritual needs of all men.

This age forces the church into a situation in which limp excuses are to be exposed, shabby veneer removed, and spiritual dwarfism rejected. The new mood of the church, not yet found in all congregations but becoming more widespread, is to be less tolerant of wishful thinking and careless planning and to condemn inconsistencies of practice in the church rather than blame "world problems." Growing maturity is sought by more leaders.

There are many signs that indicate that this could be the most creative day in New Testament history. The Spirit moves in many hearts and stirs many souls to restlessness. Men who are weary of the shabby ethics which surround their daily work are ready for the church's vital challenge. There is an impatience toward any longer languishing in the prison of selfishness which looks for returns on the investments of love, which specifies standards of love to be kept and averages to be met. Christian love that comes from an inexhaustible Source wants to spend and to be spent, dares to be reckless and be loosed for the true ministry designed for it by the Suffering Servant Himself. Stewardship programs should allow the free flow of divine love which meets the tearful needs of the masses, invites, and challenges a surging love to break forth beyond the limited vision of men. The response of love reaches far beyond churchly concerns, through the community and nation to the entire world.

God's dynamite is available to blast the way to build new stewardship roads for carrying more freight. Stewardship activities can show the vistas of God, lead to new frontiers of witness and service to humanity. This is the maturity we seek.

Whatever We Plan to Do, Let Us Do It Now

"Stand fast in the Lord" (Phil. 4:1). "They that wait upon the Lord shall renew their strength, they shall mount up with wings as eagles, they shall run and not be weary, and they shall walk and not faint." (Is. 40:31)

God will supply all our real needs! He said so!

Notes for Chapter 9

[1] John Bright, *The Kingdom of God* (Nashville: Abingdon Press, 1953), pp. 265, 266.

[2] E. J. Friedrich, "Toward the Preservation of Our Evangelical Heritage," *The Cresset*, XXVI, No. 10 (October 1963), 6.

Bibliography

Bibliography

Books

Azariah, V. S. *Christian Giving*. New York: Association Press, 1955.
Baillie, D. M. *God Was in Christ*. London: Faber and Faber Ltd., 1961.
Beck, W. F. *The New Testament in the Language of Today*. St. Louis: Concordia Publishing House, 1963.
Bonhoeffer, Dietrich, *The Cost of Discipleship*. Macmillan Co., 1960.
Brattgard, Helge. *God's Stewards*, trans. Gene Lund. Minneapolis: Augsburg, 1963.
Bright, John. *The Kingdom of God*. Nashville: Abingdon Press, 1953.
Byfield, Richard, and James P. Shaw. *Your Money and Your Church*. Garden City, N. Y.: Doubleday & Co., Inc., 1959.
Caemmerer, Richard R. *Preaching for the Church*. St. Louis: Concordia Publishing House, 1959.
Coleman, Robert E., *The Master Plan of Evangelism*. Westwood, N. J.: Fleming H. Revell Co., 1963.
De Dietrich, Suzanne. *The Witnessing Community*. Philadelphia: Westminster Press, 1958.
Edge, Findley B. *A Quest for Vitality in Religion*. Nashville: Broadman Press, 1963.
Elert, Werner. *The Christian Ethos*, trans. Carl J. Schindler, Philadelphia: Muhlenberg Press, 1957.
Franzmann, Martin H. *Follow Me: Discipleship According to Saint Matthew*. St. Louis: Concordia Publishing House, 1961.
Heimarck, Theodore. *Preaching for the Tethered Man*. Minneapolis: Augsburg, 1962.
Henderlite, Rachel. *A Call to Faith*. Richmond: John Knox Press, 1955.
———. *Forgiveness and Hope*. Richmond: John Knox Press, 1961.
Henry, Carl F. H. *Christian Personal Ethics*. Grand Rapids, Mich.: Wm. B. Eerdmans Publishing Co., 1957.
Kantonen, T. A. *A Theology for Christian Stewardship*. Philadelphia: Muhlenberg Press, 1956.
———. *Resurgence of the Gospel*. Philadelphia: Muhlenberg Press, 1948.
Kauffman, Milo. *The Challenge of Christian Stewardship*. Scottdale, Penn.: Herald Press, 1955.
Keech, William J. *The Life I Owe*. Valley Forge: Judson Press, 1963.
Koeberle, Adolf, *The Quest for Holiness*. Minneapolis: Augsburg Publishing House, 1938.
Kretzschmar, Karl. *The Stewardship Life*. St. Louis: Concordia Publishing House, 1929.
Kuntz, Kenneth. *Wooden Chalices*. St. Louis: Bethany Press, 1963.
Laymen's Movement, The. *Living My Religion on My Job*. New York: Wainright House, 1962.
Lindemann, Paul *Christian Stewardship and Its Modern Implications*. St. Louis: Concordia Publishing House, n. d.

185

Marty, M. A. *The Hidden Discipline*. St. Louis: Concordia, 1963.

McKay, Arthur R. *Servants and Stewards*. Philadelphia: Geneva Press, 1963.

Pinomaa, Lennart. *Faith Victorious*. Philadelphia: Fortress, 1963.

Ralston, Holmes. *Stewardship in the New Testament*. Richmond: John Knox Press, 1946.

Reinhart, Bruce. *The Institutional Nature of Adult Christian Education*. Philadelphia: The Westminster Press, 1962.

Rice, Brian. *What is Christian Giving?* London: SCM Press, 1958.

Ritchl, Dietrich. *A Theology of Proclamation*. Richmond: John Knox Press, 1963.

Schweizer, Eduard. *Church Order in the New Testament*. London: SCM Press, 1959.

Shedd, Charlie W. *How to Develop a Tithing Church*. Nashville: Abingdon Press, 1961.

Thielicke, Helmut. *The Freedom of the Christian Man*. New York: Harper & Row, 1962.

————. *The Waiting Father*, New York: Harper & Brothers, 1959.

Thompson, T. K. *Christian Stewardship and Ecumenical Confrontation*. National Council of the Churches of Christ, Department of Stewardship and Benevolence, 1961.

Thurneysen, Eduard. *A Theology of Pastoral Care*. Richmond: John Knox Press, 1962.

Walther, C. F. W. *The Proper Distinction Between Law and Gospel*, trans. W. H. T. Dau. St. Louis: Concordia Publishing House, 1929.

Wingren, Gustav. *Luther on Vocation*, trans. C. C. Rasmussen. Philadelphia: Muhlenberg Press, 1957.

Magazines

Caemmerer, Richard R. "Friend and Fighter," *Concordia Theological Monthly*, XXXIV, No. 10 (Oct. 1963).

Coiner, Harry G. "The Secret of God's Plan," *Concordia Theological Monthly*, Vol. XXXIV, No. 5 (May 1963).

Grumm, M. H. "Motivation in Paul's Epistles," *Concordia Theological Monthly*, Vol. XXXV, No. 4 (April 1964).

Huldschiner, Robert E. "The Lay Perversion of the Church," *The Lutheran Quarterly*, Vol. XIV, No. 3 (Aug. 1962).

Malik, Charles. "The Gospel and the Life of the Spirit," *The Christian Century* (Aug. 23, 1961).

Sources for Materials

Church-Craft Pictures, Inc., 4222 Utah, St. Louis, Mo. 63116.

American Lutheran Publicity Bureau, 2112 Broadway, New York, N.Y. 10023